ISBN 978-1-332-59834-2
PIBN 10017240

For support please visit www.forgottenbooks.com

English
Français
Deutsche
Italiano
Español
Português

www.forgottenbooks.com

Mythology Photography **Fiction**
Fishing Christianity **Art** Cooking
Essays Buddhism Freemasonry
Medicine **Biology** Music **Ancient
Egypt** Evolution Carpentry Physics
Dance Geology **Mathematics** Fitness
Shakespeare **Folklore** Yoga Marketing
Confidence Immortality Biographies
Poetry **Psychology** Witchcraft
Electronics Chemistry History **Law**
Accounting **Philosophy** Anthropology
Alchemy Drama Quantum Mechanics
Atheism Sexual Health **Ancient History**
Entrepreneurship Languages Sport
Paleontology Needlework Islam
Metaphysics Investment Archaeology
Parenting Statistics Criminology
Motivational

Raffaello Piccoli

Benedetto Croce

An Introduction to his Philosophy by

Raffaello Piccoli

With a Foreword by
H. Wildon Carr

Jonathan Cape
Eleven Gower Street, London

Printed in the U.S.A.

FOREWORD

THIS book is the account of the life and activity of one who is living and acting. Herodotus tells us the Greeks had a proverb which forbade them to pronounce any man happy before he is dead. We may certainly take his warning to this extent,—that we should refrain from attempting to fix a philosopher's thought so long as he continues to think. Benedetto Croce has, it is true, presented his Philosophy of Mind in such "questionable shape," that it gives the student the impression of finality, the feeling that a doctrine which throughout the history of philosophy has been struggling for expression has now at last come to light. But this appearance of finality is due to a certain artistic power which Croce possesses in an eminent degree, the power of reliving the past and making history interpret life. Beneath all his systematization there is the germ of a new life, a new life, which, will take form in new problems. While then we may say that no living philosopher has given so complete an appearance of finality to his doctrine as Croce has done in his *Philosophy of Mind* it is really the reflection of a work of art which serves only to conceal the living thought.

Foreword

The publishers of this Introduction to the philosophy of Benedetto Croce by Dr. Raffaello Piccoli have courteously invited me to write this foreword inasmuch as I was the first to introduce this philosophy, otherwise than by translations, to the attention of English students. I do so very gladly. My own work was confined to the purely philosophical writings, my interest in them having been first aroused by the striking address on Aesthetic delivered by Croce to the International Congress of Philosophy at Heidelberg in 1908. When I wrote my book, the *Philosophy of Mind* consisted of three volumes, the *Estetica*, the *Logica*, and the *Pratica*, but before I had completed my account I read in Croce's Journal *Critica* the announcement of the forthcoming publication of the fourth volume on the *Theory and History of the Writing of History*. Croce had, it seemed to me, closed his book on *Practice* with the plain indication, not that he had solved every philosophical problem, nor that philosophy was not an external problem, but that he had given an exhaustive account of the stages or degrees in their order as moments of the developing life of the mind, and that outside these degrees there were no others. The new work did not, indeed, either negative or qualify this conclusion, but it bore evidence of the ceaseless activity of his mind. Are we then, because the philosophy of Croce is still

ERRATUM

Foreword, p. 2, *line* 21.   *For* external *read* eternal.

developing, to refrain from the attempt to interpret it on the ground that any meaning we may find in it is indefinite and insecure? Certainly not, for a philosopher's thinking unfolds and develops like a living thing, it is not constructed like a building, nor does it rest on foundations which may be unsound.

Dr. Raffaello Piccoli, a professor in the University of Pisa, and the author of this book, was born in Naples, Croce's city, in 1886. He himself as a young student came under the personal spell of the philosopher he writes about, and grew up in the intellectual atmosphere which his philosophy was creating. To this great advantage he has added another, for first in Australia, and later in the Universities of England and America he has acquired a perfect command of our language and a thorough knowledge of our philosophy. He is specially qualified, therefore, to give a first-hand account of Croce's literary and philosophical activity, and the kind of influence it has had in forming the mind of Modern Italy.

The author has not confined himself to an exposition of the philosophy of Croce in its narrow and technical meaning, he has given us an account of the whole of his literary and historical activity. He has traced the origin of his philosophy in the circumstances of his parentage, early life and education, and has followed biographically the formation of his philosophical theories and the direction of his philosophical interest. He has shown how his general trend of thought, his literary tastes and historical studies without any professional spur, by the very nature and force of the problems with which they confronted him, led to philosophy as the dominant and culminating interest of life.

Philosophers and philosophies have had in our generation to undergo the trial of a fiery furnace. The Great War and the passions aroused by it and the estrangement between nations nurtured in the same Western culture have been a fierce test of principles. In regard to every great leader we ask first how he reacted to the conflicting emotions of the international struggle. Dr. Piccoli has dealt with this latest and crucial period of Croce's activity in a very sympathetic spirit. Croce's attitude at one time exposed him to an extreme unpopularity. This was largely the result of misunderstanding. He has come through the ordeal with enhanced reputation. This, at least, is the author's judgment—the judgment of one who himself fought and suffered severely in the War.

The two great achievements of Croce are in the domain of aesthetical and ethical theory. Dr. Piccoli shows us each doctrine in its historical origin and in its relation to contemporary philosophy. The first is a reaction against the intellectualism of Hegel. In its affirmation of intuition it is in rather striking agreement with the philosophy of Bergson, although as Croce's approach is from the side of art and literature, and not like Bergson's from the study of biological science, it rather supplements than elucidates Bergson's theory. The second is a reaction against the school of Karl Marx and its materialistic interpretation of history.

At the present time Croce is directing his criticism on the new line of development which his own friends and colleagues are taking in regard to his own principles, in particular to the "actual idealism" of his colleague Professor Giovanni Gentile. To Croce this new doctrine spells mysticism, and of mysticism in all its forms he is the open enemy. On this point we may, I think, detect an inclination on the part of Dr. Piccoli to disagree with Croce. It will be seen, therefore, that we have in this book a very full and a very welcome account, brought right up to date, of one who is, as far as contemporaries can judge, forming the mind of the present age.

H. Wildon Carr

PREFACE

WHEN, about a year ago, I undertook to write this little book for its present publishers, all that I had in my mind was a brief exposition of the solutions given by Croce to a number of philosophical problems of vital interest to the students of what were once called the Moral Sciences. I thought at the time that it would be possible to abstract such solutions and problems from the body of his Philosophy of Mind, which is a coherent and austere theory of knowledge of a kind that in the modern decadence of philosophical studies and of general culture is rapidly becoming unintelligible even to the most highly cultivated. I hoped that the specialized reader, for whom the larger aspects of Croce's thought have no appeal, and therefore no meaning, would be able to apply those particular solutions to the problems that confronted him in his particular branch of studies, by translating them into terms of his own naïve philosophy.

This plan had also a personal advantage, inasmuch as it did not compel me to a conscious revision of my own position in regard to those larger aspects of Croce's philosophy. But as soon as I began to think consistently of this book, the history of my own reactions to Croce's work came back to me so vividly that I found it impossible to set it aside; and I discovered that this supposed advantage was a delusion, towards which I had probably been drawn by a very human, very natural desire of avoiding the most obvious difficulties of my task.

As a young man, in my student days in Italy, I was a fervid and enthusiastic follower of Croce's ideas: one of the many who used to swear, as we were wont to say, *in verba Crucis*. To the generation who opened the eyes of their intellect in the dawn of the century, he had revealed what seemed to be the only safe path between the two precipices of a pseudo-scientific materialism on one hand, and of a mysticism on the other, which in all its many forms (traditionalism, modernism, pragmatism, intuitionism, æstheticism, super-humanism, futurism) could not be anything less than an abdication of thought for the sake of the emotions. And it should not be wondered at, if Croce's books, appearing at short intervals between 1900 and 1910, and building up what presented itself to us as a complete system of answers to all, or practically all, our most pressing spiritual questions, were received by us with deep gratitude but with very little constructive criticism. They covered such an enormous space on the map of European culture, that even for the most ambitious among us, they were very often the first introduction to entirely new fields of studies, and all we could do was to follow our guide in his voyages of rediscovery:

to repeat within ourselves the strenuous experience of which each of those books was a report and a testimony.

Impatience with a master who was not of the kind we had been accustomed to, who could not be easily digested, surpassed and disposed of, but had as much energy and courage, as light a step and as curious a mind, as the most gifted among his pupils, prompted a good deal of immature and capricious criticism, which was but a means for an arbitrary liberation. It was an amusing sight to see Croce assailed and, to the satisfaction of his critics, destroyed, with weapons that nobody could have provided but Croce himself, and a dwarf victoriously brandishing against the giant a toothpick for a sword. But there is no epic of thought without such comic interludes.

My own faith in Croce was not shaken until intercourse with one of the greatest critical minds of our day, and the representative of a totally different philosophical tradition, a mathematician and a philosopher, showed me the weakness of the foundations not of Croce's, but of my own idealism. And a long residence in England, where I became intimately acquainted with certain logical habits utterly unlike our Latin ways of thought, made me profoundly sceptical of the intellectual advantages of whatever dogmatism might have been in me. Yet I continued for a long time to keep as it were in separate compartments those that had seemed to me to be established truths in Croce's system, and speculations of a quite different order on problems which were forced upon me by my own experience of life and by contact with a new moral and cultural environment.

All this was in the happy days of peace. The war from its very beginning appeared to me, then living in one of the most purely intellectual centres of Europe, at one of the oldest Universities of England, as the catastrophe of our whole intellectual life. From the trials of the war I emerged with infinitely less faith in the value of our intellectual possessions than I ever had had before, and at the same time with the firm conviction that intelligence, more intelligence, a deeper, purer, more active, charitable, courageous and pervasive intelligence, is our only hope for the future.

It was with such a disposition that I took up this work, and read what Croce had been writing during the war. Three things, in the course of this new acquaintance with him, and while I was meditating and lecturing on him during my American peregrinations, became very clear to me. The first, that his thought is not a system in the ordinary sense of the word, but a method; that therefore it is impossible to sever parts of his philosophy from the main body, the truth of particular propositions being dependent upon an understanding of the whole.

The second, that in the last few years the progress of his thought has been so considerable that an at-

tempt at giving a general exposition of his philosophy
without any regard to the successive stages of growth,
at describing as a static structure what is a dynamic
process, would inevitably lead to the construction of
a fanciful system, of an image totally different from
the original.

The third, that whatever our individual position
may be in relation to his ideas, his work before, during and after the war will remain as the most solemn
contemporary monument of that intellectual civilization of Europe, of which we have seen so many false
idols, so many white sepulchres, go under during
these seven years of passion.

The conclusion to be drawn from these considerations was obvious: first, that I had to give up my
former plan, and this with no regret, as I ought to
have remembered what Croce has taught again and
again, that to the naïve philosophy of the specialist
his own solutions of his particular problems, however
childish they may appear from a higher standpoint,
are perfectly adequate, that ready-made, formal solutions are no solutions at all, and the only truth is the
one that we conquer by our own effort, under the
impulse of our own need. And second, that, however conscious I was and am of my own limitations,
I had to take a first step in the direction of constructive criticism by trying to retrace the history, the
ideal biography, of the philosophy of Croce.

With the exception of a little book written by
Croce himself, there is very little help to be found

for a work of this kind in the vast literature that has grown in the last twenty years, in Europe and in America, around his work. And I firmly believe that there is not one man in Europe or in America who is qualified to do that work of creative interpretation which ought to be at the same time a history and a criticism of Croce's philosophical activity: least of all, the professional philosopher, who has dealt all his life with the conceptual residuum of the problems of life, and has no direct experience of any of them. Croce, as this little book will try to show, has always come to the concept from the concrete, particular problem, and has occupied himself with such a variety of problems, going into them so deeply and so thoroughly, that a complete valuation of his work will never be possible to a single man, but will *take place*, will *happen*, in the history of the various disciplines, and in the general history of thought, for years and years to come. For the present, and as long as he will be alive and thinking, the only creative interpreter of Croce is Croce himself.

This book does not therefore intend to substitute itself, not even as a summary and a short cut for lazy minds, to the works of Croce. It is rather an introduction to those works, and at the same time the confession of one individual experience of that philosophy. It is an historical sketch, and implicitly a criticism, since our way of understanding a thought is our judgment of that thought (when not a judgment that that thought passes on us); a sketch which

I think I can honestly write because so much of that philosophy has been the daily food of my intellectual life, my own history, for years. Before the war I should probably have been able to write it with less difficulty, with more complete adhesion; but the perspective of these few years will make it perhaps less passionate and more reflective. An explicit criticism of the whole philosophy of Croce it is not, and it does not attempt to be: the reader may find traces of my doubts and of my preoccupations in it, but I have humbly tried to give not more, and I hope not less, than what he has a right to expect from the title.

I do not write this book for the professors of philosophy. Those among them who know Croce will not need it; and those who either have not as yet taken any notice of him, or from a casual acquaintance with one of his books have proceeded to damn most vigorously what they have hardly understood, are certainly beyond my power. I write it for the young, from the heart of my own now fast receding youth, trying to raise before their eyes, in the words of Dante to Brunetto Latini,

la cara e buona immagine paterna
di voi, quando. . . . . . ad ora ad ora
m'insegnavate come l'uom s'eterna.

I trust that they will find in it what they need not less than we of an older generation needed it, and what I know they are thirsting for: an example of intellectual energy and of moral strength converging into a life of unremitting devotion to the service of that truth which is light and love and joy,—our only light against the menace of darkness.

RAFFAELLO PICCOLI.

NORTHAMPTON, MASS., June–October, 1921.

BENEDETTO CROCE

INTRODUCTION

I. THE BEGINNINGS

BENEDETTO CROCE was born in 1866, in a small
town in the Italian province of Aquila, the only son
of an old-fashioned, Catholic, and conservative Neapolitan family. His grandfather had been a high
magistrate, untouched by the new liberal currents
in his devotion to the old régime and to the Bour-
bon dynasty then reigning in Naples. His father
followed the traditional maxim of the "good people"
of Naples: that an honest man must take care of his
family and of his business, and keep away from the
intrigues of political life. His mother was a woman
of culture and taste, such as the old type of education
for women, which is now as completely forgotten as
if it had never existed, used to produce. Bertrando

Spaventa, the philosopher, and Silvio Spaventa, a statesman who had brought to his enthusiasm for the national cause all the traditions of his Neapolitan conservatism, were her brothers: both of them, however, estranged from Croce's family because of their political ideas.

The child grew in this greyish, subdued atmosphere, in which the only touches of colour were added by his own passion for books of history and romance, and by the visits to the beautiful old churches to which he accompanied his mother. To the circumstances of his childhood, Croce attributes the relative delay in the development of his political feelings and ideals, for a long time submerged by his interests in literature and erudition. But because every fault brings with itself some compensation, he also owed to them his critical attitude towards partisan political legends, his impatience towards the rhetoric of liberalism, his vehement dislike of great emphatic words, and of any kind of pomp and ceremony, together with a power to appreciate what is useful and effectual in the actions of men, wherever it may come from.

As a boy, he went to a Catholic "collegio" or boarding school, and in this too his experience differed from that of the majority of his contemporaries. The insistence on lay education imparted by the State, and the preference for the day school, which allows the family to supplement the work of the school, in fact, to take care of the moral and social side of education, as distinct from the purely intellectual one, are characteristics of the new Italian methods, obviously in keeping with the general tendencies of the age. I remember that to myself as a boy it was inexplicable why anybody should be sent to a "collegio," unless he were an orphan or an unmanageable scamp. But Croce seems to have enjoyed his experience, to which he was submitted merely in accordance with the habits of his family; and even now he praises the system for breeding in him those feelings of loyalty and honour, which are the result of life in common with boys of one's own age, and of the necessity of adapting oneself to a variety of dispositions and temperaments.

Classical secondary education in Italy roughly corresponds in its scope, even to-day, to that which is imparted in Anglo-Saxon countries by secondary schools and liberal colleges. It is supposed to end the "formative" phase of education, and to lead to the higher phase in the Universities, which is, whether cultural or professional, of a highly specialized and "informative" kind. It is the direct outcome of the humanistic tradition, and rather more so in the clerical schools, like the one which Croce attended, than in the public ones. By the time he was ready for the University, he must have had a good knowledge of the classics, as a general background to a mainly literary and historical culture, in which the elements of scientific knowledge, and a good deal of mathematies, had also their place.

The religion which played such an important part

in his family and school life was probably little more than a habit with him: a set of answers to certain fundamental problems which, accepted on the authority of parents and teachers, released his mind for the pursuit of his favourite studies. And yet, there is no doubt that we can find traces of this religious education in all his work: a personal experience of the catholic catechism and of catholic morality brings a spirit in contact with some of the great ideas and of the great realities of life in a much more intimate and profound way than the purely intellectual apprehensions of the same ideas and realities ever will. It creates habits of mind and moral tastes which will still be recognizable even after the individual mind to which they belong has undergone the most radical changes. In a philosopher, in particular, it forms a kind of personal background to thought, similar to that which modern philosophy actually has in its own history: it reproduces in the youth of one man that religious phase which corresponds to the youth of a civilization, and is the source of the intellectual development of a more conscious age.

At intervals during his adolescence, Croce's faith intensified itself into passing aspirations towards a life of devotion, until it quietly vanished, so to speak, from his consciousness, through no great dramatic crisis, but merely in consequence of a course of lessons on the philosophy of religion, which were intended to strengthen it and make it more resistent to criticism, during the last years of his secondary education. At about the same time, having come under the influence of both Carducci and De Sanctis, he began to write, and contributed his first articles to a literary weekly, the *Fanfulla della Domenica*, which represented the most vigorous and advanced tendencies of the day.

In 1883, in the earthquake of Casamicciola, in the island of Ischia near Naples, Croce lost both his parents and his only sister, he himself remaining buried for several hours under the ruins, and broken in several parts of his body. The years immediately following were the "saddest and darkest" of his life, and he spent them in Rome in the house of his uncle Silvio Spaventa, which was one of the most conspicuous political and intellectual centres of the capital of the new kingdom. Spaventa was one of the leaders of the Right, or Conservative party, which had been thrown out of office by the Left, or Liberal party, a few years before; by him and by his friends the young Croce was strengthened in his mistrust of the prevailing ideas and methods, which he heard bitterly and sarcastically criticised by men of great culture and of profound political honesty. While his temperament and the shadow of his grief kept him away from the brilliant social life of the Roman *jeunesse dorée*, his relations with the men of a party which had little hope of ever coming back to power prevented him from taking any part in active political life, in sharp contrast with the habits of the majority of Italian university students, to whom politics are what the major sports are to Anglo-Saxon students. He divided his time between the University and the great Roman libraries, among which the one he loved best was the Casanatense, in those years still served by Dominican monks, a typical old monastic library, its benches provided with old-fashioned inkhorns, sandboxes with golden sand, and goose-quills. Anyone seeing him there, buried among his ancient and curious books, and not suspecting the deep perpetual dissatisfaction and un-happiness which accompanied him in a work which seemed to be but a work of love, would have proph-esied for him the life of one of those ascetics of erudi-tion, intoxicated by the romantic dust of the past, who still haunt the solemn halls and the dark corri-dors of the libraries of the old world.

But the great event of his University life, the one which awakened him from the torpor of mere erudi-tion, and set before him a new goal and a higher hope, was the lessons on moral philosophy which he heard from Antonio Labriola. Croce himself has de-scribed this new, decisive experience: "Those lessons came unexpectedly to meet my harrowing need of rebuilding for myself in a rational form a faith in life, and in the aims and duties of life; I had lost the guidance of a religious doctrine, and at the same time I was feeling the obscure danger of materialistic theories, whether sensistic or associationistic, about which I had no illusions at all, as I clearly perceived in them the substantial negation of morality itself, resolved into a more or less disguised egotism. Herbart's ethics taught by Labriola restored in my mind the majesty of the ideal, of *that which has to be* as opposed to *that which is,* and mysterious in its opposition, but because of this same mysteriousness, absolute and uncompromising." [1] Labriola's influence on Croce was not limited to the classroom; the professor and the student became friends, and Croce enjoyed the benefit of his wonderful gifts as a conversationalist, on which even more than on his academic activity, or on his published work, his fame rests. He seems to have been an awakener of souls, an intellectual stimulant in the fashion of the Greek philosophers, a breaker of new paths and a spiritual guide such as a younger generation had in the mathematician Vailati.

The mind of the young scholar is henceforth constantly occupied by meditations on the concepts of pleasure and duty, of purity and impurity, of actions prompted by the attraction of the pure, moral idea, and of actions which result in apparent moral effects through psychic associations, through habits, through the impulse of the passions. It is easy to discover the dependence of such meditations on the early religious education of Croce; they are the link, in fact, between his religion and his philosophy, since we find them, at a more mature and elaborate stage, reflected in the third volume of his *Philosophy of*

---

[1] *Contributo,* pp. 21, 22; and *passim,* pp. 1–30, for practically the whole substance of this section.

Mind, which, to the eyes of its author, has still an almost autobiographical aspect, entirely concealed from the reader by its didascalic form.

The plan of life that he sketched for himself about this time, was a distinctly disillusioned and pessimistic one: on one hand, he would pursue his erudite and literary work, partly because of his natural inclination towards it, and partly because one has anyhow to do something in this world; and he would, on the other hand, fulfil his moral duties to the best of his capacity, conceiving them to be above all *duties of compassion.* In later years he criticised this view as a purely selfish one, since "the true and high compassion is that which one practices by setting the whole of one's self in harmony with the ends of reality, and by compelling others too to move towards those ends, and a kind heart makes itself truly and seriously kind only through an ever broader and deeper understanding." [2]

After three years of residence in Rome, Croce returned to Naples, where he lived in the society of curious and learned old men, librarians and archivists, all absorbed in minute and painstaking historical researches. The moderate fortune which he had inherited from his parents gave him the independence he needed for his quiet, laborious tastes, and allowed him gradually to collect in his own house a very large and precious library. To it he owed also the possibility of learning without teaching, and therefore of

[2] *Contributo,* p. 23.

keeping his own work entirely free from any academic taint: of subordinating his studies rather to the necessities of the development of his own personality than to those of professional specialization.

Practically all the production of the years between 1886 and 1892 is concerned with one aspect or another of the history of Naples. Through his researches on the Neapolitan theatres, on Neapolitan life in the eighteenth century, and on the literature of the seventeenth century, he acquired an intimate and exhaustive knowledge of the minutest literary, political, social and archæological details of that life of his own city, which was the immediate historical background of his own life. Towards the end of this period, this complex activity crystallized itself into two rather ambitious enterprises: the editing of a *Biblioteca letteraria napoletana,* for the publication of texts and documents of Neapolitan literature; and of a periodical, *Napoli Nobilissima,* which in the fifteen years of its existence collected an enormous amount of material for the history and archæology of Naples, and to which Croce himself contributed the essays of his *Storie e leggende napoletane.*

We have here a Croce, who, though not a professor, was yet truly a specialist: one of that great host of local and municipal historians which are to be met with in even the least important Italian towns. And undoubtedly this kind of activity offered him, as he willingly acknowledges, not only an outlet for his youthful imagination, in the reconstruction of an adventurous and picturesque past, but a formal discipline of precision and thoroughness in scientific work. But it must be remembered that municipal or regional history in Italy has in many cases the breadth and depth of national history in other countries, because of the number and variety of divergent political, literary and artistic traditions which are present in the life of each Italian city or state. And Naples, though she never had as preponderant a part in the formation of the national consciousness as either Rome or Florence, was a world in herself, with her own art and poetry, with her own philosophical and political tendencies, with her peculiar relations to non-Italian states and cultures, such as France and Spain. Croce's Neapolitan researches, however specialized and barren they may appear at first sight, were therefore well fitted to give him, in one particular instance, that direct and concrete experience of historical reality, of a complex and variegated historical reality, which is among the necessary premises of his philosophical thought. They gave him also a clearer consciousness of the processes of thought which were naturally connected with that particular experience, and they thus helped him to penetrate the minds of his two great Neapolitan predecessors, Vico and De Sanctis. And finally, especially through his interest in the cultural relations between Naples and Spain, they enlarged his horizon from the problems of local to those of general European history.

He visited, always as a scholar, not only Spain, but France and England and Germany, constantly widening the range of his excursions in libraries and archives. But the more he acquired of the knowledge of individual facts, the deeper he felt the futility and vacuity of their purely material accumulation. There was no end, apparently, to the labor of research and erudition, unless a guiding and limiting principle should be found: by the mere piling up of historical information, however minute and exact, it would be forever impossible to decipher the secret of the past. No amount of erudition would ever make history. It is no wonder that to a mind which already had been preoccupied with religious and moral problems, the problem of its own work should present itself with the same intensity and in the same shape as a moral experience. He began to feel a satiety and distaste for that which he had once thought would be the labour of his whole life, and a yearning for a more satisfying, more *intimate* form of activity. He felt a vague attraction towards a new type of history, moral history, in relation to which all his previous researches appeared as a kind of amorphous and unconscious preparation. He planned a book on the psychological and spiritual history of Italy from the Renaissance to our own times, and he undertook a series of studies on the relations between Spain and Italy, to be followed by similar work in regard to the other nations of Europe, as necessary to a full understanding of his main theme.

But his old methods and habits followed him in the new field: again it seemed to him that there would be no end to his merely preparatory work, once he had undertaken it in what was practically still his old spirit. In fact he had sensed a spiritual need which had announced itself by that peculiar feeling so closely resembling one of moral dissatisfaction, but he had not been able as yet to formulate the terms of his problem. It is probable that what kept him for quite a long time from doing so was partly the character of his literary education, and partly a kind of intellectual humility, which made him distrust his own powers, on entering into a completely new form of mental activity.

*T*he problem which he had to solve for himself was, indeed, not an historical, or philological, or archæological one, but a purely philosophical one: the problem of the nature of history and of science. We know with what religious awe Croce regarded the professional philosophers at the time; and certainly nothing could have been more painful to the young and modest scholar than the thought of stepping beyond the limits of his own specialty, and invading a ground so powerfully occupied and defended. But Croce discovered through his own experience that you cannot reject a problem, once it is forced upon you by the facts of your own life, and that *philosophus fit* with the same kind of necessity with which *poeta nascitur.* It is from this point that we can observe the transformation of the young scholar into a philosopher; his philosophical career will appear to us as a continued effort towards the solution of that first problem, and of all the problems which followed in its train. The last answer to it is in Croce's theory of the identity of history and philosophy; and the dependence of this theory on the first impulse from which the whole of his philosophy arose is clearly visible in the desire which he has again and again expressed and partly fulfilled in his latest writings, of going back from abstract and formal philosophy to the philosophy of particular facts or history: *storia pensata;* "since this is the meaning of the identity of philosophy and history, that we philosophize whenever we think, whatever may be the subject or form of our thought." [1] The philosophy of Croce, which begins with the raw material of history, presenting itself as a dense, impenetrable mass, ends in a new conception of history, which is permeated in all its parts by the vivifying breath of thought.

I may add here, since it will be very hard to interrupt the history of his intellectual development with biographical details, that the new direction of his thought did not alter Croce's external mode of life; that the discipline acquired in his early work remained the norm of all his later activity; that he accepted public offices in his own town, and later as a senator (which in Italy is a life-office) and as a Minister of Public Education in the last Giolitti

[1] *Contributo,* p. 81.

Cabinet, certainly more out of the consciousness of a moral obligation than through his inclination or his ambition. His life on the whole has been and is essentially that of the scholar and of the thinker: his work, a political work only in the wide meaning which Plato gives to the word.

II. EARLY ENVIRONMENT

Benedetto Croce was thirty-four years old in nineteen hundred: his education (if it is possible to set a term to the education of a philosopher) is therefore the work of the last quarter of the nineteenth century. A rapid examination of the intellectual conditions of Italy during those years will help us to see that education in its true light, that is, as a reaction to, rather than a fruit of, the environment.

The Risorgimento, with its fifty years of wars and revolutions coming close on the heels of the great Napoleonic upheaval, left Italy materially and morally exhausted. After centuries of foreign domination, of political and spiritual servitude, all the elements of Italian culture had been gathered by the two generations of the Risorgimento into a new culture, which was much more an instrument of combat, for the conquest of unity and independence, considered as the necessary premises of national life, than the best soil for the spiritual growth of that life after the conquest. This new culture, in the poets who had announced and formed it, Parini, Alfieri,

Foscolo, Leopardi, Manzoni, in its philosophers, Rosmini and Gioberti, and in its prophet and apostle, Mazzini, had forms and spirits, the value and meaning of which by far transcended the importance of its immediate historical purpose; but through the difficulties and labors of the practical effort, it reached the end of the period shorn of a good deal of what was deepest, most beautiful, nearest to the universal, in it. Italy in 1870 was very much like the sprinter who wins the race, but collapses at the crossing of the line.

The culture of Italy had been for centuries oscillating between the pursuit and discovery of certain universal values, which had gradually become part of the common European culture (the Roman idea, the Christian idea, the main principles, æsthetic and moral, of the Renaissance), and the development of purely local, regional characteristics. At the end of the Risorgimento, the links that had kept Italian culture in constant contact with the rest of Europe were broken, and on the other hand the local cultures found themselves, as it were, lost and submerged in the new political readjustment, threatened in their very existence by the new claim of loyalty advanced by a literary and abstract national ideal. The duties of Italian culture, clearer to us now than to the men who lived in the midst of those events, were then, on one side, to re-establish the connection between Italian and European culture, and this time more by learning than by teaching—and on the other side to utilize the less particular elements of the regional cultures as a foundation for a real and concrete and diffused cultural life in the nation.

Thus Italy becomes, at the beginning of her new, unified existence, little more than a province of European thought. She looks around herself and she is compelled to take notice of what had happened beyond her frontiers during the last two or three centuries. It is interesting to compare the characteristics of the other great nations of Europe as they appear to Italy during and after the Risorgimento. England, who had been a symbol of political liberty, a source of political and economic wisdom, reappears as a model of industrial development and at the same time as the proclaimer of a new creed to the world, the creed of evolution, which after having infused a fresh spirit in the natural sciences with Darwin, seems to promise a new interpretation of human life, a new organization of science and of social thought, with Spencer. France, the mother of revolutions, the deliverer of the spirit of man from the shackles of divine and earthly tyranny, remains, in a vague and hazy fashion, through the many disappointments that her policies give to her Italian lovers during all this period, the same kind of inspiration that she has been ever since the Encyclopédie and the Revolution; but contributes to the new effort little more than her veristic fiction, in which art itself is reduced to a handmaid of the goddess of the hour, biological and social science.

Germany had saturated with the romantic atmosphere of her poetry the passionate struggle of the times, and she had captured a little band of thoughtful patriots, among whom we find Croce's uncle, Bertrando Spaventa, with the fascination of her new metaphysics, in which they found the fulfilment of all the promises of Italian thought in the foregoing centuries; but after her victory over France, the same cause that makes French influence less vigorous, makes also German influence less deep and less inspiring. A Germany who has like Faust sold her romantic and metaphysical soul, yields only a shadow of her great historical and philosophical culture of the eighteenth and of the first half of the nineteenth century, though a tremendously powerful one, and such that for a long time it overawes the academic mind not of Italy only, but of the whole continent. A narrow and materialistic philology, under the name of historical method, becomes the heir to the humanistic tradition, and substitutes itself for every native impulse, even in fields in which Italian thought had been master for centuries, as in that of law: where it mercilessly destroys, of the ideologies of the Risorgimento, not only that which was arbitrary and fanciful, and therefore destined to perish, but even that which through the subsequent course of history was to prove vital and sound. The Italian school of international law, the new conception of the Law of Nations, for instance, which was the fruit of the Italian juridical tradition during the experiences of the Risorgimento, and which is the more or less consciously accepted foundation of all the doctrines of international relations striving for realization in our times, in no country and in no schools was so resolutely repudiated as in the Italian universities. And it could not have been otherwise, since the new philology was as static and deterministic a doctrine, only more logically and rigorously so, as the evolutionary positivism which we had learnt from England.

The faults of Italian culture during this period are therefore the faults of the other European cultures which Italy had to assimilate: at a time when Italy was most in need of cultural help from without, she found that, for reasons infinitely complex and totally different from those which had caused her own exhaustion, the other nations of Europe were also spiritually exhausted. And yet it cannot be said that from these very faults Italy did not draw some useful lessons. The so-called historical method, which completely disregarded the great forces of history, and made of the least significant historical datum a *Ding an sich* in which the mind of the scholar seemed to find its ultimate object, proved in the end to be a salutary discipline as against the facile and enthusiastic generalizations of the historians of the Risorgimento. Positivism, however barbarous and uncouth in itself, was a powerful weapon for the destruction of the last remnants of a more or less mythological metaphysics, and in that sense it afforded an example

of intellectual honesty; and at the same time it awakened the consciousness of the continuity of natural
and spiritual life, announcing, though in a hasty and
imperfect synthesis, what every philosophy of the
future will have to be. And about the middle of the
period which we are now considering, the only real
contribution of Germany to European thought in the
second half of the century became known in Italy
with the advent of Marxism, in which we found a
new conception of history, in so far adequate to the
true spirit and conditions of the times, as it afforded
to blind social forces, striving for political expression,
an interpretation of their needs and a rationalized
programme of action.

The analogies between this general cultural atmosphere, and the present conditions of the intellectual world in America, are, provided we do not
stress them too hard, so striking that I cannot refrain
from calling the attention of the reader to them. I
believe this will help him to apply a good many of
Croce's criticisms and ideas to tendencies and problems with which he is thoroughly familiar. The most
recent forms of American philosophy, pragmatism,
instrumentalism, realism, are indigenous elaborations
of that same English positivism and empiricism
which was dominant in Italy a generation ago: the
relations between science and philosophy are seen
in the same light in America to-day as in Italy before
the beginning of this century. And the two most
significant and far-reaching directions of research,

social psychology and psychoanalysis, branching out into every ramification of social and moral and æsthetic thought, are based on assumptions, and lead to results, very similar to those of the Spencerian sociology and of the Lombrosian theory of insanity and genius. Even in fiction America is to-day trying her hand at verism, and in poetry, apart from a few marked exceptions, she is experimenting in the same spirit in which we began to follow, about the end of the period, the most recent fashions of Paris in vers-librism and decadentism. In academic circles German philology has maintained its sway for a much longer time than in Europe, and the war has brought about more an emotional than an intellectual consciousness of the need of a vaster and deeper understanding of history. Finally, certain aspirations towards ancient and totally different systems of moral and æsthetic standards, embraced with an enthusiasm that is akin to an act of faith—the hope to discover a refuge and a consolation from the chaos of modernity in a restoration of classical or mediæval ideals—are American varieties of an attitude of mind which found its satisfaction in Italy in patterns which we drew after the models of Ruskinism and of French traditionalism.

On the whole, Italian culture was suffering from the effects of the same delusion which accounts for the straits in which American culture is to-day: that European culture could be assimilated through its representatives at one particular moment only, and as if it were at the surface of time, rather than by the only legitimate and fruitful method, which is that of delving beneath that surface for the truly fundamental contributions that each nation has made to the common mind. Not one of the nations of Europe was then, or is now, at one of those turning points in the history of culture in which principles of universal value are elaborated within the limits of a single national group. The only possible exception was that of Russia, sending out to an age-worn Europe a fresh message of human pity and Christian love in a succession of epic masterpieces; but the quality of the message was such as to affect the heart much more than the intellect, to produce a new and deeper feeling rather than a sounder knowledge.

Two great individual figures, however, dominate the whole period, and among so many contrasting currents of thought and feeling, among the fluctuating fashions of the times, connect the new generations with the traditional elements of Italian culture. That breadth of vision, that sense of the perspective of history, which was totally lacking in the prevailing cosmopolitan thought, was a conspicuous characteristic of the work of a great critic, Francesco de Sanctis, and of a great poet, Giosuè Carducci. And what made the secret of the strength of the one as well as of the other, was their fidelity to the regional traditions from which they were issued, coupled with a power to invest them with a much broader significance than they had ever possessed. With De Sanctis, the speculative trend of the Southern Italian mind, with Carducci the humanism of Florence and Tuscany, for the first time in history become real elements of a greater national consciousness. Neither the one nor the other was, moreover, without a knowledge of, and a taste for, foreign cultures; but what they gained from these were elements of more permanent value than the ones which attracted 'the attention of the crowds, and they both succeeded in grafting those foreign elements on their native dispositions in such a way and with so little violence that they seemed to belong rightfully to them. This is true of what De Sanctis learnt from the idealistic philosophers of Germany, and particularly from Hegel, as well as of what Carducci acquired from the great poets and historians of the two previous generations in France, in England, and in Germany. Nor should we marvel at this, since by going deep enough or high enough into any of the European cultures, it is always possible to find a level that is common to all of them.

Francesco de Sanctis was not a philosopher in the strict meaning of the word; yet, among all the European critics of the nineteenth century, he is the only one from whose works it is possible to derive a consistent line of æsthetical thought. His education had been partly philosophical, of old Italian and modern German philosophy; and partly grammatical and rhetorical, in those literary doctrines of the old school which embodied a secular experience, and in compari-

son with which the modern *science* of literature is
ineffably shallow and puerile. It was through a
philosophical elaboration of those doctrines, and
through a criticism of the intellectualistic æsthetics
of Hegel and his followers, for whom art was the
sensuous clothing of the concept, that De Sanctis,
guided by an unerring taste and by a unique power
for discerning the essential and vital element in
poetry, came to his conception of form as not an *a
priori*, a thing by itself and different from the content, but something that is generated by the content itself when active in the mind of the artist.
This is the principle which he had constantly in mind
in approaching the concrete works of poetry, and
which enabled him to analyze and reproduce the
terms of the spiritual experiences of which they are
an expression. Thus his *Essays* and his *History of
Italian Literature*, though in a sense the purest and
most genuine kind of literary criticism, are at the
same time a complete spiritual history of a people,
as it reveals itself in its literary manifestations, such
as no other country possesses. The immediate influence of his work was not as great as it ought to
have been: the generation of philologists who immediately followed him was unable to see in him
more than a brilliant exponent of what was then
contemptuously called æsthetic criticism, and could
never forgive him for his apparent lack of method,
due to the circumstances of his life as an exile and a
politician. It was only unwittingly, and through the

intermediary of a German disciple of De Sanctis, Gaspary, who wrote a standard handbook of Italian literature, that they came to accept the greatest part of his interpretations, and followed the main directions of his thought in their own researches.

Giosuè Carducci was a disciple of Parini and Alfieri, of Foscolo and Leopardi, and in a sense of all that lineage of Italian poets, beginning with Dante and Petrarch, for whom poetry was not less an arduous discipline for the attainment of a certain standard of formal beauty, set down once and forever by the poets of the classical tradition, than a moral and political function in the life of the nation. As his predecessors had been, he was not only a poet, but also a student and historian of literature, of literature as the only field in which that life had truly realized itself. But though his contributions to the study of Italian literature were many and important, and the knowledge and taste which were the instruments of his art made of him an exquisite critic of poetry, yet what even in his historical and critical prose attracts us most is his lyrical imagination, his poetry. And his poetry, on the other hand, is mainly the poetry of the history and of the historical and poetical landscape of Italy,—of an Italy which was to him not merely one among the nations of Europe, but the heir of Greece and of Rome, the cradle of western civilization; not a land and a community limited in space and in time, or not that only, but an ideal of beauty, of freedom, of right, of a full and harmonious life, which was Italian, as it had been Greek and Roman, because it was universally human. In his early works, the contrast between this ideal and the actual conditions of Italy in his times found expression in a strain of invective and satire, from which the poet lifted but rarely his soul to the contemplation of the great deeds and thoughts of the past; of a past which in some cases was very recent, as some of the men of the French Revolution and of the Risorgimento were among his favourite heroes. But later, and especially in his *Odi Barbare*, for which he adapted a new technique from the metres of ancient Greece, while he added many personal notes to his lyre, his historical inspiration became higher and deeper and purer, and Italy had in his poetry that which she had lacked in all the course of her literature, a true *epos*, though in a lyrical form, of her secular life, from the fabulous kings and priests of Etruria to that most legendary of all her heroes, Garibaldi.

The influence of Carducci, not a purely literary, but a moral and political one, on the generation to which Croce belongs, can hardly be overestimated; and Croce himself calls his own generation *carducciana*. And the two other great poets that Italy has produced after him, D'Annunzio and Pascoli, were both disciples of Carducci at the beginning of their careers. But the formation of their personalities, so widely divergent in their later developments, is contemporaneous with what we have called the education of Croce, and therefore outside the scope of this rapid review of the circumstances under which that education took place. The growth of the erotic-heroic poetry of D'Annunzio and that of the idyllic-humanitarian poetry of Pascoli are no longer among those circumstances but rather products of the same environment.

III. The Origins of His Thought

There are philosophers for whom it is possible, and relatively easy, to trace the roots of their speculations and of their systems in the thought of one or a few predecessors. The research of what we might call their sources, or more precisely of the terms in which certain problems were handed down to them through the particular philosophical tradition to which they belong, would probably not lead us very far in space or very deep in time: it might be useful in such cases to preface the history of their thought by a brief summary of these immediate antecedents. But in the case of Benedetto Croce, such a summary ought to extend, in relation to the problems in which he is or has been interested, to the whole range of the history of human thought. This is due partly to his peculiar approach to the problems of philosophy, and partly to his method of work.

Philosophy is to him neither a special science nor a specialized technique: not a discipline which requires a scholastic training, and which you can definitely acquire after a given number of years of study, but just what it was in the beginning: that love of wisdom which prompts every man to the exercise of his thinking powers. The problems of philosophy cannot be enumerated and defined, but that which happens to you, or your own doings, in your life, in your conduct, in your work, in your study, is the perpetually renewed material for your meditation. Problems are not given to you from outside, as puzzles at which you might try your skill or duties imposed by a pedagogue: they are your experience, and your philosophy is your conscious logical reaction to them.

This unprofessional and broadly human view of philosophy was not, however, an obvious and spontaneous attitude of Croce's spirit, but a laborious conquest. In the years of his erudite and unphilosophical youth, at his first coming in contact with philosophy in the strict and technical meaning of the word, with philosophical treatises and dissertations, his attitude was one of profound respect for the professors of philosophy, "as I was persuaded," (he tells us in his autobiographical notes), "that they, as specialists, should possess that abstruse science, of whose sacred curtain I had hardly lifted a few folds, and I did not know that in a few years I should with wonder and irritation discover that most of them did not possess anything, not even that very little which I, merely by my good will to understand, had succeeded in acquiring." [1] The fact is that these pro-

[1] *Contributo*, p. 26.

fessors and specialists could hardly be termed philosophers at all, while Croce had already in himself that
obscure and tormenting desire for intellectual clarity,
which is the beginning of philosophy.

But in this initial ignorance, in his coming as if
unaware to the gates of the temple, we shall find the
reasons of Croce's method of work. When a given
problem presents itself to him, not as a subject of
learned controversy, but as a spiritual necessity, he
becomes suddenly conscious of the duty of following
the history of that particular problem through centuries of thought. The first impulse may come from
a mere attempt at understanding the terms under
which the problem presents itself to him: a clarification of words. His mental habits are, in fact, those
of the conscientious and painstaking philologist, and
he brings the method and discipline of the severest
erudition into the field of logic. There is no problem
for him that is purely logical, in an abstract and
formal sense; still less, purely psychological. The
mere occasion for his speculation is sometimes offered, as we shall see, by contemporary discussions,
but he feels from the very beginning that these discussions are merely concerned with the surface of
things, are taking place on a plane of thought, mechanical and dilettantesque, on which all conclusions
are equally legitimate and equally irrelevant. Very
soon, and long before any trace can be found in his
writings of his final identification of philosophy with
history, he practically identifies each problem with

its own history, by retracing, generally in an inversely chronological order, the original meanings of terms and theories of which contemporary culture gave him only a pale and distorted reflection.

But this intimate and vital contact with the past never leads him to that attitude of reaction, which our forefathers typified in the *laudator temporis acti*, and which even to-day is so abundantly exemplified by the scholar who, having laboriously climbed the heights of the thought of one man or of one epoch, feels himself in the possession of final truth, and smiles contemptuously on the childishness of the moderns. He is as much on his guard against the idols of the school as against the idols of the market place. His relation to the great thinkers of the past is not one of blind discipleship, but of critical collaboration. The favourite process of his own thought might be defined as one of historical integration.

By emphasizing one aspect or another of Croce's philosophy, it is possible, however, to connect him more particularly with one or another philosopher. The name that is most frequently pronounced in this connection is that of Hegel, probably because Hegel stands, in the mind of the positivist and of the pragmatist, for a certain type of thought, much more ancient than Hegel himself and practically coextensive with the history of philosophy, rather than for what Hegelianism actually is. The facile critic of Croce, who condemns and rejects him as a Hegelian, would probably find it very hard to define the actual points of contact between the two thinkers; but we know that the word "Hegelian" is more a term of abuse, in such cases, than the expression of a critical judgment. Croce himself has defined his attitude towards Hegel, and generally towards the philosophers of the past, in the conclusion of his examination of Hegel's thought: "I am, and I believe one has to be, Hegelian; but in the same sense in which any man who to-day has a philosophical mind and culture, is and feels himself, at the same time, Eleatic, Heraclitean, Socratic, Platonic, Aristotelian, Stoic, Sceptic, Neoplatonic, Christian, Buddhist, Cartesian, Spinozian, Leibnitzian, Vichian, Kantian, and so on. That is, in the sense that no thinker, and no historical movement of thought, can have passed without fruit, without leaving behind an element of truth, which is an either conscious or unconscious part of living and modern thought. A Hegelian, in the meaning of a servile and bigoted follower, professing to accept every word of the master, or of a religious sectarian, who considers dissension as a sin, no sane person wants to be, and no more I. Hegel has discovered, as others have done, one phase of truth; and this phase one has to recognize and defend: this is all. If this shall not take place now, it matters little. 'The Idea is not in haste,' as Hegel was wont to say. To the same content of truth we shall come, some day, through a different road, and, if we shall not have availed ourselves of his direct help, looking back on the history of thought we shall have to proclaim him, with many an expression of wonder, a forerunner." [1]

This last hypothesis describes what actually happened in the case of another among the ancestors of Croce's Philosophy of Mind. For two centuries either unknown or misunderstood, Vico came into his own only a few years ago, and mainly through the efforts of Croce himself. In Vico, that is in Italy at the beginning of the eighteenth century, practically all the germs of the idealistic philosophy, and of the historical and critical culture of the nineteenth century, were already present, as a natural development of the philosophical and humanistic Renaissance. And it is through what, in Vichian style, we may call the discovery of the true Vico, that Croce inserts himself in the central tradition of Italian, and European, culture, and is saved from the dangers inherent in his catholic attitude towards the philosophers of the past, that of a material, mosaic-like eclecticism on one side, and that of a metaphysical syncretism, such as led Hegel to the dialectic constructions of his Philosophy of History, on the other.

The philosophy of the Renaissance, in which the fundamental impulses that are the soul of that movement find their clear and distinct expression, had produced a new naturalism and a new spiritualism with Giordano Bruno and Tomaso Campanella: that is, two widely divergent views of reality, which however had sprung from a common source, the opposi-

[1] *Hegel*, pp. 147-8.

tion to that scholastic synthesis in which all the transcendental elements of Greek and Roman philosophy had been gathered to the support of mediæval theology, in direct relation with the mediæval description of the cosmos. There has probably never been made in the world, either before or after the Middle Ages, such a resolute and comprehensive attempt at an intellectual understanding of the moral and material universe, as the one that is the work of mediæval philosophy: but that attempt had been made possible, and had brought definite results, only through the acceptation of the limits of revealed truth, which, however freely accepted, proved in the end to be much more compelling than to the modern scientist are the freely accepted limits of external reality. Revealed truth could not be a mere object of thought, as it carried within itself, under the mythological disguise, its own metaphysics and its own ethics: a new principle, in fact, a more absolute and intimate spirituality than had been known to either the Greeks or the Romans, which attracted to itself all the kindred elements in ancient thought, and determined the essential characteristics of mediæval speculation.

The discovery and establishment of this spiritual principle, as a universal reality which transcends nature and the spirit of man, and which to this natural and human world is as a law dictated from outside and from above, is the message of the Middle Ages, not in pure philosophy only, but in religion and ethics, in science and in the life of society. The Renaissance is the beginning of our modern world, inasmuch as it is, through the infinite variety of its artistic, social, religious, scientific manifestations, an effort to see that same spiritual principle no longer as a transcending reality, but as the active, immanent, all-pervading soul of immediate reality, both natural and human. The Ptolemaic cosmography, which is the visible form of mediæval thought, a system of the finite universe, of which the Earth is the centre, and which leaves an infinite space for the seat of the only real, transcending existences, beyond the compass of the heavenly spheres, and as if it were outside itself, loses its hold on the imagination, and therefore on the conscience of men, long before Copernicus and Galileo read in the skies a new system of an infinite universe, within which, or nowhere, the divine principle must live and work.

The impulse towards the identification of the spirit with nature, on one side, and with man on the other, had been at work in Italian life and thought all through the Renaissance; but it is only at the end of that miraculous spring of Western civilization, between the close of the sixteenth and the beginning of the seventeenth century, that it expresses itself in the philosophies of Bruno and Campanella. Bruno presents himself as an expounder and defender of Copernican astronomy, and Campanella writes the apology of Galileo. And to each of them the scientific discoveries are much more than mere helps and suggestions for metaphysical speculation; they are the revelation, in one field of human thought, of a new logic which has to be recognized, in one form or another, as the fundamental principle of modern civilization.

Both in Bruno and Campanella, inert remnants of the ancient and mediæval logic are still part of the structure in which their new intuitions try to express themselves; but such remnants are to be met with even in much later philosophers, and constantly re-appear, as blind spots in the active process of thought, in the whole history of European philosophy down to our days. What is significant of each thinker, what marks him as the legitimate interpreter of the deepest spiritual life of his times, is not his system as a whole, but the particular new intuition on which in each case the system is founded: in Bruno, the conception of an infinite universe, and of the infinite life of God in the universe; in Campanella, the af-firmation of the value of human experience and hu-man consciousness, to which God is present *per tactum intrinsecum*, intrinsically, and in which know-ing and being coincide.

The two main directions of modern thought, or rather of all human thought, are thus represented in the naturalism of Bruno and in the spiritualism of Campanella, at the conclusion of the Renaissance, respectively prefiguring the pantheism of Spinoza and the rationalism of Descartes, that is, the two systems through which similar conceptions became active and effective in all subsequent developments of European philosophy. And it is useful to recall their names as an introduction to the exposition of the ideas of a modern Italian philosopher, because we are to-day only too prone to identify certain forms of common European thought, originating from Greece and from Italy, with what was only their last expression in the great idealistic movement in Germany in the nineteenth century; where Bruno and Spinoza reappear in Schelling, and Campanella and Descartes, through the intermediary of the English thinkers of the eighteenth century, in Kant and Hegel.

I am not trying to establish an Italian pedigree for the kind of philosophy to which Croce belongs: nowhere are national distinctions so futile as in the history of thought. But the Italy of the Renaissance shares with India and with Greece the purely material privilege of having given birth to a vision of the world and its problems, which is national only in the sense that it was elaborated for a certain time at least by minds belonging to a single nation. The value of that vision, however, does not reside in any tribal or national characteristic, but in those elements of universality, which made of the Italian culture of the Renaissance, and of its inherent logic, the basis of all modern European culture. What can still be recognized as peculiarly Italian, or French, or English, or German in the thought of modern philosophers, is not that phase of truth, which may be present in it, but the element of prejudice, of crowd-mindedness, of spiritual inertia, which even the greatest among them have in common with their weaker brothers.

In Bruno and Campanella we find an interest in certain problems of thought, which we may call either religious or, more technically, ontological: the problems of the relations of being and knowing. In Vico, who is infinitely nearer to Croce in intellectual temper, the centre of interest is shifted. Vico is apparently satisfied with Catholicism as a religion; and he spends all his efforts in creating a philosophy out of the purely humanistic and historical side of Renaissance culture. And yet, long before Kant's *Prolegomena*, he foresees the necessity of the new metaphysics being the metaphysics, as he says, of human ideas, and his theory of knowledge is founded on a principle which bears an external resemblance to certain aspects of pragmatism, but is in reality of a quite different, and much deeper, character: that of the interchangeability of the *factum* with the *verum*, of that which we make with that which we know. It was a commonplace of the schools that perfect science is to be found in God only who is the author of all things: Vico transfers this logical formula from God to man, and applies it, in the first stage of his thought, to mathematics, which appears to him as of man's own *making*, in a narrow and abstract sense, and later to the whole world of history and human thought and action, which, in a much truer and broader sense, is *made* by man.

Vico was brought to this second and final form of his theory of knowledge by his studies on the history of law, of religion, of language and poetry: his philosophy is essentially a philosophy of the moral sciences, of philology in its widest meaning. And the whole of his speculation, in his *Scienza Nuova*, takes the shape of an enquiry into the origins and development of human society: not essentially of a sociology, an empirical and inductive science of man (though this aspect is undoubtedly also present in his mind), but rather, through "the unity of the human spirit that informs and gives life to this world of nations," of an ideal and eternal history of mankind, a philosophy of the human mind.

A contemporary and an antagonist of Descartes, Vico is one of the last among European philosophers to embrace practically the whole range of contemporary culture. But while Descartes lays the foundations of his theory of knowledge on the certainty of mathematical method, mistrusting the imperfection and vagueness of any other form of science, Vico is enabled by his intimate contact with rhetoric and history, with that *philology* which had been the soul of the intellectual life of the Renaissance, and which through the erudition of his century was preparing the historical consciousness of the following one, to anticipate the general principles of idealistic philosophy and, on the theories of art, of language, of law, of religion, as well as on a large number of particular historical problems, the general development of subsequent European thought.

At a later stage in our exposition, we shall examine in greater detail the indebtedness of Croce to Vico,

especially as regards the theory of art and language;
but the similarities of circumstance and of temperament between the two philosophers are already apparent.   Both Vico and Croce came to philosophy
through erudition and philology; and in Croce as
well as in Vico, the fundamental philosophic attitude,
their theory of knowledge, their idealism (what in
the case of Croce has been called his Hegelism), is
the intrinsic and necessary logic of the same humanistic tradition, the natural outcome of the centering
of their intellectual interests on the history of the
human spirit rather than on the mathematical or
natural sciences.   It is only after Descartes and Vico,
and through the independent progress of scientific
thought in the last two centuries (during the Renaissance, science is constantly in contact with philology,
and there is no scientist who is not also a humanist)—
that the two divergent attitudes of mind which we
have seen exemplified in Bruno and Campanella,
naturalism and spiritualism, are finally divorced from
each other, and respectively linked with the scientific
or with the historical aspect of modern European
culture.   Rationalism, intellectualism, positivism,
pragmatism, on one side, are the more and more
rarefied logics of science, in its progressive estrangement from the humanities; and because of the in-
creasing prestige of scientific thought, we see them
making constant inroads even in the fields of the
historical and philological disciplines.   Idealism, on
the other side, represents in its many forms the

central tradition of European culture, and is heir to
the religious thought of the Middle Ages as well as
to the humanism of the Renaissance; but in many of
its exponents, and to my mind, even in some aspects
of Croce's philosophy, it suffers from that same condition of things which is the cause of the poverty
and narrowness of the so-called scientific philosophies:
from that inability to grasp both nature and the
spirit of man, the world of science and the world of
history, which is a characteristic of our times. The
recurrence of the realistic position, after every great
affirmation of idealistic philosophy, is certainly not
the mere recurrence of error, the obstinate perma-
nence of human folly after the pronouncements of
wisdom, but rather the restatement of a logical exi-
geney which cannot be entirely satisfied and disposed
of by any of the idealistic solutions of the problem
of reality. Idealism and realism in modern philosophy are two distinct and divergent elaborations of
different fields of modern culture: that unity of the
intellectual vision, which is perfect, within its accepted limitations, in mediæval philosophy, and
which is never entirely lost sight of in the thought of
the Renaissance, is the goal towards which both
realism and idealism continually tend, but which will
not be reached by either, until the *disiecta membra*
of our intellectual consciousness will be brought together through a higher synthesis than the one from
which they fell apart at the end of the Renaissance.

We are now in a position to understand why it would be vain to look in the work of Croce for either an organized synthesis of scientific thought, understood as a means through which the mind of man grasps the reality of nature, or a system of metaphysics attempting to explain the facts of our human life by reference to an order of superhuman and supernatural realities. These are two types of philosophy, a criticism of which is implicit in every step of Croce's philosophical career, as well as in the quality of his philosophical ancestry. But in their place we shall find a series of meditations on the problems of the human spirit in its actual historical development; on the distinctions and inter-relations of the various forms of spiritual activity, not as they appear, in a purely abstract and external consideration, to the eye of the psychologist, but as they reveal themselves in the intimacy of those spiritual and historical processes, in which man creates at the same time his own being and his own truth. As we have stated already, the philosophy of Croce is essentially a philosophy of the humanistic tradition, of that Italian and European tradition the consciousness of which seems to be fast disappearing even among those who consider themselves as its exponents and defenders; and which in his thought not only justifies and understands itself, but brings that justification and that understanding to a greater depth, to a more comprehensive clarity, than it ever reached during the many centuries of its existence.

PART FIRST
FROM PHILOLOGY TO PHILOSOPHY
(1893–1899)

I. HISTORY AS ART

CROCE'S first philosophical essay is a short memoir, *La Storia ridotta sotto il concetto generale dell' Arte*, which he read to the Accademia Pontaniana of Naples in March, 1893. In his autobiographical notes, Croce tells us that this memoir was sketched by him one evening in February or March of the same year, "after a whole day of intense meditation." [1] But the reader cannot help feeling that those few pages are very far from being an improvisation; and this, not only because of the ease with which the author finds his way among the literature of his subject, but especially because one realizes that only a discipline so constant and so severe as to become a kind of second nature could give him that sure grasp of the essentials of his problem, which he shows from the very beginning of his speculation. The majority of historians and philologists, when they turn their attention to what Croce calls the logic of their discipline, are apt to trust themselves exclusively to their

[1] *Contributo*, p. 32.

45

immediate experience of their work, and to disregard the very obvious fact that an inquiry into the general principles of a certain branch of knowledge is, and cannot be anything but, philosophy: they are therefore either unwilling or unable to follow the implications of that logic on to their ultimate consequences, as this operation would inevitably lead them away from their own safe and solid ground into a discussion of unfamiliar concepts and ideas. They seem to perceive but dimly that the problems of that logic have been intimately connected with the whole development of philosophical thought from the Sophists to our day; and therefore even when they go back to philosophical authorities in their treatment of these problems, when they quote Plato or Aristotle, or Leibnitz or Hegel, they are content with mere fragments, arbitrarily understood, unconnected with the general body of thought from which they derive their meaning. The result is, at best, a futile rediscovery of truths and truisms which have their place in the history of thought, but are meaningless in their modern context. An examination of the greatest part of the methodological literature of the last fifty years, both in Europe and in America, would easily bear out this contention: that it is hard to find a more shallow and imcompetent philosophy than that of the average historian and critic.

What saved Croce from the academic weakness

which seems to be congenital to this kind of lucu-
brations was, besides the native temper of his mind,
an instinctive realization of the true philosophical
import of the problems involved. The question,
whether History is an art or a science, had been a
favourite one with the generation to which Croce's
masters belonged; and it was really threatening
to become an endless, insoluble one, since no attempt was ever made to solve it by the only method
which could give positive results, that is, by an
accurate definition of the concepts of both art and
science. The most common answer to it, and the
one that most clearly proved the confused state of
mind of those who formulated it, was that history
was at the same time a science and an art. The
traditional humanistic view, which considered history as one of the arts, and to which the inclusion
of Clio in the college of the Muses bears witness,
found but little favour in a time which was entirely
under the domination of the pseudo-scientific
philosophy of Herbert Spencer, and could therefore hardly admit of any form of knowledge which
was not scientific knowledge. The third solution,
history as a science, was in fact the most usually
accepted one, being but one aspect of that general
tendency of the age, superficial and uncritical,
through which all forms of knowledge were striving
hard to assimilate themselves to the mathematical
and natural sciences. This tendency which was
present in all fields of philology, manifested itself

in history either in the attempt to transform history into sociology, and to substitute a system of
institutional schemes or of so-called general laws
for the actual historical processes, or in the raising
of the usual canons and criteria of historical method,
that is, of a collection of maxims and precepts for
the proper handling of sources, documents, and
monuments, to the dignity of a supposititious science.
It is characteristic of Croce, that he did not directly
attack the English and French and Italian sociologism which was so popular in his day: to a mind
which had received its first logical training at the
hands of a Thomistic schoolmaster, and had been
introduced to modern philosophy through Labriola's
Herbartism, the logic of the average sociologist was
so abhorrent in its barbarity, that it did not even
afford him a starting point for his own criticism.
The fallacy of sociologism is made evident in the
course of the discussion, but rather by implication
than through a direct animadversion. He chose his
own adversary among the exponents of the other
form of the same error, among the German critics,
whose ideas were more clearly defined and logically
more consistent.

Their main position can be stated in a few words:
history is a science and not an art, because its aim
is not to give æsthetic pleasure, but knowledge. The
premises of this formula are a hedonistic conception
of art, and the identification of all forms of knowledge with science: that is, a too narrow definition

of art, and a too broad definition of science. Croce's demonstration takes the form of a rigorous syllogism: he defines the concept of art and the concept of science, the two definitions forming so to speak the two horns of a dilemma; history is shown by its own definition to be included in the definition of art, and the only remaining question is that of the distinction, within the same concept, between art in the strict sense and history.

The most important part of this demonstration is that which concerns art. Croce's object was to discover the nature of history, but his real achievement in his first essay was that of stating the æsthetic problem in its true terms. His opinions about history and about science were destined to undergo many changes in the further development of his thought; but his whole theory of æsthetics is already virtually present in these few pages about art and the Beautiful.

"Art is an *activity* aiming at the production of the Beautiful." [1] A purely psychological doctrine of æsthetics, which considers not art as an activity, but the objects of art as a collection of stimuli, a doctrine of æsthetic appreciation rather than of æsthetic creation, of the kind that has flourished in Germany and in England during the last twenty years, especially in the field of the graphic and plastic arts, will therefore be incapable of even grasping that which is the specific subject of æsthetics. But Croce does not

[1] *Primi Saggi*, p. 8.

lose his time in attacking the psychologists. The error
of their ways has its philosophical expression in Sensualism and in Formalism, which he summarily dis-
misses together with Rationalism or Abstract Idealism: the Beautiful as pleasure, the Beautiful as a
system of formal relations, the Beautiful as abstractly
one with the Good and the True. The fourth solution of the problem of the Beautiful, which he accepts, is that of the Concrete Idealism of Hegel and
Hartmann: the Beautiful as *expression*, as the sensuous manifestation of the ideal. But Croce was
guided by his Latin moderation (and probably also
helped by his, at the time, insufficient understanding
of German Idealism) to give to this formula not the
intellectualistic interpretation which rightly belongs
to it, but the very simple meaning of an adequate
and efficacious representation of reality. The difference between this conception of Art—as an activity aiming at the representation of reality—and
the one that we shall find in Croce's later elaborations
of his æsthetic theory, does not lie in the conception
itself, but in its context of general thought. Here he
is still working under the common-sense assumption
of a double reality, of being and of thought, and this
explains why he still speaks of form and content, and
why he still admits of a category of Beauty of nature
side by side with artistic Beauty. Later, the relation
between form and content will transform itself into
that of the æsthetic activity with the other forms of
spiritual activity; but even such a momentous change

in the foundations of his theory does but slightly impair the substantial truth of the words in which he first expressed it: "An object is either beautiful or ugly according to the category through which we perceive it. Art is a category of apperception, and in art, the whole of natural and human reality—which is either beautiful or ugly according to its various aspects—becomes beautiful because it is perceived as reality in general, which we want to see fully expressed. Every character, or action, or object, entering into the world of art, loses, artistically speaking, the qualifications it has in real life, and is judged only inasmuch as art represents it with more or less perfection. Caliban is a monster in reality, but no longer a monster as an artistic creation." [1] As to natural Beauty, Croce observes that it is not inanimate, as Hegel and his followers would have it, but animated by the spirit of the beholder, and its contemplation is therefore a kind of artistic creation: [2] but this observation, in which the later doctrine is present in germ, is set forth timidly in a note, and remains for the moment sterile and as if incapable of yielding its obvious logical results.

If it were admitted that history is a representation of reality, its inclusion in the concept of art would be obvious. But the adverse contention is that history is a scientific study of reality, or to use Bernheim's definition, the science of the development of men in their activity as social beings. Croce's answer

[1] *Primi Saggi*, p. 14.   [2] *Primi Saggi*, p. 14n.

is that history is not a science, because history is constantly concerned with the exposition of particu-lar facts, and not with the formation of concepts, which is the proper sphere of science.   There may be a science or philosophy of history, investigating the philosophical problems connected with the facts of history, but such a science or philosophy, which can-not be distinguished as a separate organism from the philosophy of reality as a whole, is not history. History does not elaborate concepts, but reproduces reality in its concreteness: it is therefore not science but art.

Sociology, on the other hand, which renounces the concreteness of history in the quest for the general laws of human development, is neither art nor science. When compared with the concepts or laws of science, the laws of sociology appear as vague and empty generalizations, and sometimes as mere pseudo-scientific enunciations of contemporary social and political ideologies.   The sociology which Croce had in mind in his criticism was, in substance, because of the fallacy of its logical premises, either inferior science or poor philosophy; but because of the un-certainty of his own idea of the relations between science and philosophy, it was easier for him to re-jcct it than to define it.   His reaction was the instinc-tive one of a sound logical organism against a mental hybrid.   He was certain that sociology, whatever else it might have been, was not history.

This part of Croce's argument is undoubtedly the

weakest. His conception of science was inadequate, and his discussion of the relations of history with science suffered from this inadequacy: the problem which he had attacked could not be solved at this stage of his speculation. While his æsthetics was contained in germ in his conception of art, his logic was not even adumbrated in his conception of science. In fact, the only real function of the latter was to mark the limits of the former: "In the presence of an object, human mind can perform but two operations of knowledge. It can ask itself: what is it?, and it can represent to itself that object in its concreteness. It can wish to understand it, or merely to contemplate it. It can submit it to a scientific elaboration, or to what we are wont to call an artistic elaboration." "Either we make science, or we make art. Whenever we assume the particular under the general, we make science; whenever we represent the particular as such, we make art." [1]

This distinction is the old Platonic one between *logos* and *mythos;* a distinction that appears in one form or another in practically every system of philosophy, but the true import of which has never been completely grasped before Vico. From Vico Croce quotes in this connection the following passage: "Metaphysics abstracts the mind from the senses, the poetical faculty must submerge the whole mind in the senses; metaphysics lifts itself above the universals, the poetical faculty must plunge itself in the

[1] *Primi Saggi*, p. 23.

particulars." [1] This quotation shows how decisive
was Vico's influence in the determination of the main
theses of Croce's æsthetics: of which we already find
here the three fundamental ones, that is, the recognition of art, or the æsthetic activity, as one of the
fundamental forms of knowledge; the distinction of
the æsthetic activity from, and its opposition to, the
logical activity; and, finally, the exclusion of any
other form of knowledge besides the æsthetic and the
logical, which exhausts the whole of man's theoretical
activity.

The rest of this particular discussion is not as
fruitful or as interesting. Having included history
in the concept of art, Croce proceeds to draw a distinction between art in the strict sense, which is a
representation of imaginary or merely possible reality,
and history, which represents that portion of reality
which has actually happened. His final definition of
history is: "That kind of artistic production the
object of which is to represent that which has really
happened." [2] The value of this definition is what
we might call a value of reaction against the pseudo-
scientific sociology of his day: it consists in the emphasis laid on the concreteness and individuality of
historical processes, against the void schematism of
general laws. But by introducing the distinction
between the possible and the real, Croce had in fact
recognized the presence of a conceptual element in
history—a conceptual element totally different from

[1] *Primi Saggi*, p. 23n.   [2] *Primi Saggi*, p. 36.

the concepts of the sciences, which were all that he could then see outside the æsthetic activity in human knowledge. In a preface to a reprint of his early philosophical essays, written twenty-five years later, Croce explained the conditions which prevented him from perceiving the new problem at once, in a page of admirable self-criticism: "Why did I not perceive it? Because I was full of the first truth which I had found, and for the moment I did not feel any other need: I had violently rejected the weight of sensism and sociologism, and I could breathe. And in my culture at that time the impulses towards that other need were lacking; because neither my scholastic logic nor Labriola's Herbartism opened my mind to a distinction between the concepts of the sciences and the speculative concept; and De Sanctis, entirely given to the criticism of poetry, gave little attention to logical problems. The authority of my first masters of philosophy induced me, in regard to the problems which I had not experienced in myself, to content myself with temporary formulas and solutions, which attracted me through some aspects of truth, and to be satisfied with an imagination of the Ideal above the real, and of the world of Concepts above the world of representations. By this separation, by this collocation in the Empyrean, it seemed to me that I could better attest my reverence for concepts and ideals, which positivists and evolutionists were dragging in the mud, or lowering to the status of superstitions and hallucinations. Now, running again through my pages, it is not possible for me to think those transcendental doctrines again, not because I thought them in the past, and what is past is past, but, on the contrary, because I did not truly think them even then, but only received them or imagined them, so that what I can think now is only the way in which, then, I was brought to imagine them, and to believe that I thought them." [1]

[1] *Primi Saggi,* pp. XI–XII.

II. ON LITERARY CRITICISM

AT the end of the following year (1894), Croce interrupted again the steady flow of his erudite production with the publication of a little book, *La Critica Letteraria: questioni teoriche*, which was the outcome of a discussion he had had during the summer with a friend, a professor of philosophy. As the net result of his first philosophical effort had been the conquest of a clearer conception of art, it was natural that he should proceed to investigate the relations between history and the subject-matter of history in that field in which he felt he had already been able to find some light. The general problem of the nature of history, of which he had seen but one aspect, was set aside for the moment, giving way to a close examination of the methods of historical thought in the study of literature.

Only a few of the conclusions of this particular research were destined to have any kind of permanency in Croce's theories; but it is useful to recall them, not only as a step in the development of his thought, but as representing a marked progress in that conception of literary criticism which is still predominant wherever the influence of that thought has not yet been felt. Croce submitted that conception to a process similar to what a French critic calls a disassociation of ideas, trying to establish which can be said to be the essential operations of literary criticism, and the relations between these and the various kinds of possible works on literary material. Given this method, which is that of abstract classification, and having approached his problem through criticism itself instead of starting from the other end and deducing the concept of criticism from the concept of art and literature, he was bound to reach a number of abstract concepts, apparently irreducible to each other, and the fundamental unity of which he could only later affirm through the general progress of his theory of æsthetics.

Literary criticism, which until fifty or sixty years ago, stood only for the judgment and valuation of literary works, to-day usually includes, beside the æsthetic valuation, the study of the historical development, the edition and comment of the text, the biography of the author, the exposition of the work itself, the æsthetic theory of literature, and so on; in fact, every kind of conceivable work on literature. The danger of this extension of meaning lies in the facility with which we are led to believe that many things, when called with one name, are really one thing: we think of literary criticism as of the synthesis of all the above-mentioned operations—a synthesis which, as Croce observes, when it exists cannot be due to anybody but the printer. Or, again, we may consider that one or another of those operations is the true aim of literary criticism—and to that one we subordinate all the others, as merely subservient to the particular aim we have in sight. This is the origin of the various *schools* of criticism—æsthetic, historical, psychological—each of which believes itself to be in possession of the only legitimate method. But if we subordinate the history of a work to its æsthetic valuation, we deny the independence and intrinsic importance of history; if we subordinate the æsthetic valuation to the historical consideration, we make of the former a useless accessory of the latter; if we subordinate the biography of the author to the historical explanation of the work, we destroy the importance of biography, which, though useful in a certain sense to the explanation of the work, is in itself "nothing but the history of the development of a moral personality." [1] In fact, the unity of literary criticism lies not in its aim, but in its subject-matter: what we mean by literary criticism is "a series of particular operations having independent aims, without any other connection than that of the material employed in each of them." [2] Croce does not deny the possibility of using the results of one of these operations for the purposes of another, but this does not change the nature of either: "the spirit of man is not divided into small compartments: all our ex-

[1] *Primi Saggi*, pp. 79–80.   [2] *Primi Saggi*, p. 80.

perience helps us in whatever work we are doing. To
understand Petrarch's poetry, it is useful either to
be or to have been in love; but it doesn't follow that
to make love and to understand that poetry are one
and the same thing." [1]

The study of the principles of literature does not
belong to literary criticism, but to Æsthetics; or, to
use Vico's distinction, not to Philology but to Philosophy. Textual criticism, and interpretative comment, are preliminaries of literary criticism, which
begins only with the contemplation or æsthetic en-
joyment of literature: that is, with that operation of
reading which is made possible through the establishment of a correct text, and by the help, when
needed, of a convenient commentary. In literary
criticism proper Croce distinguishes three successive
phases, or moments, answering respectively to the
questions: What have I read? What is the value of
that which I have read? Which is the genesis and
fortune of this particular work? The first is the exposition or description—which in itself is a work of
art of which another work of art is the subject; the
second, the valuation or æsthetic judgment; the third,
the history of the work under consideration. Outside these three moments or phases, Croce does not
admit of any other independent critical operation:
the research of the sources of a work is only part of
the history of that work; comparative criticism is an
instrument of historical criticism; philology in the

1 *Primi Saggi*, p. 82.

strict sense of the word can in turn be used as a help
to each of the three main operations, but when it is
exclusively concerned with the general history of a
language, it is no longer a literary discipline; bibliography is a mere external element of the history
of the work; the study of the content is a literary
study only if it is pursued in relation with either the
exposition, valuation or history of the work, that is,
when the work itself is viewed as literature, and not
as a document for the purposes of another science or
discipline; the biography of the author is an element
of the genesis of the work, and therefore of its history, but its main interest is moral and not literary.

It is easy to see that, however fruitful as a reaction
to the prevailing confusion, this abstract partition
was still very artificial; but it was impossible for
Croce to go beyond it, with the help of the mechanical
and unhistoric logic which was his only instrument
at that time. He still divided a fact from its genesis,
and the fact and genesis from the judgment, and
therefore it was impossible for him to see that the
internal history of a work *is* its true exposition or
characterization, and that such characterization is
one with the valuation. In regard to the valuation
itself, he considered it to be purely subjective and
relative, as he was unable to accept either Kant's
theory of the objectivity of taste, because of its intellectualism, or the psychologists' childish delusion
of the possibility of drawing a normal or standard
taste from the average of the æsthetic likings and

judgments of different communities and different ages; and on the other hand he was still very far from discovering that identity of the æsthetic judgment with the æsthetic activity, which was to be the foundation of his later doctrine.

The discussion that follows, on the relations between the æsthetic judgment and the history of a work of art, obviously suffers from the impossibility of drawing useful consequences from a distinction of purely abstract concepts; from the fact that that which was Croce's only real discovery at the time, his conception of art, had not yet been thought out by him in the fulness of its relations with the other activities of the human spirit. As regards history, this little book is a step forward because it is a valid criticism of a confused and naïve state of mind, in which these abstract concepts could help to introduce some sort of order and method; but, on the whole, though it clarifies the terms of the general problem, it does not bring it appreciably nearer to a solution.

Croce was, however, more or less consciously aware of this deficiency. In a long *excursus* on De Sanctis, whose work he upheld as a model of perfect literary criticism, he insisted on the importance of a sound theory of art, such as De Sanctis undoubtedly possessed, as an essential part of the mental equipment of a literary critic; and the chief reproach that he addressed to his contemporaries in the field of literary studies in Italy, was that of neglecting those theoretical problems to which very little attention had been paid in our country after the work of Vico. He pointed to the great development of æsthetic studies in Germany during the nineteenth century, and affirmed the necessity of "dismissing every spirit of impatience and false pride, and of submitting oneself to the hard labour of extracting the essence of the abundant literature created by the philosophic activity of the Germans around those problems." [1] His final words contained at the same time an appeal and a programme of work: "There is a good deal to be expected from a work especially directed towards these two points: to banish a series of concepts which have introduced themselves in æsthetics, and which are entirely foreign to it, and with their presence maintain an invincible confusion; and to free the concept of art and of the Beautiful from the limits within which it has been circumscribed by linguistic habits, acknowledging the intimate connection between the so-called æsthetic and artistic facts and other facts of the life of the spirit." [3] That his attitude towards the later German æsthetics was, from the very beginning, a critical one, is clearly shown by what immediately follows: "Working in this direction, I believe that we shall find ourselves, with a new consciousness and with a wealth of observations gathered in the course of a century, to the point from which modern Æsthetics started, to the school of Leibnitz and Wolff, and to Baumgarten's conception," [3]—that is, to Baumgarten's *Meditations* of

[1] *Primi Saggi*, p. 163.   [2] *Primi Saggi*, p. 164.   [3] *Primi Saggi*, ib.

1735, in which the word *Æsthetica* appears for the first time as the name of an independent philosophical discipline, contrasted to Logic in the same sense in which the Greeks used to contrast *aistheta* to *noēta*, the facts of sensuous knowledge to the facts of mental knowledge. Which means that Croce believed the science of Æsthetics to be still in its infancy, and to require a great creative effort which was well worth making, both for the sake of the general philosophical problems involved, and for the effects that a deeper view of those problems could not but have on the practical work of the literary critic and of the historian.

Through these first discussions, which at the time appeared to him more as acts of personal liberation than as the beginning of a philosophical career, Croce had really discovered his vocation. From De Sanctis he had learnt that "art is neither the work of reflection and logic, nor the product of craft, but a pure and spontaneous *forma fantastica*": [1] through his own experience of dry erudition, and through his meditations on the relations between history and criticism, he had verified the validity and usefulness of De Sanctis' conception, and had been made aware of the necessity of doing what De Sanctis had not been either willing or capable of doing: "of creating a philosophy where he had given nothing but critical essays and delineations of literary history, and a new criticism, a new historiography, as a consequence

[1] *Contributo*, p. 54.

of the philosophic deepening and systematization of his thought." [1]

But from Croce's published work at this time it would be easy to gather the fallacious impression that his interest was an exclusively literary one: that he proceeded to create a philosophy of literature and art, and that only through the necessities of the system he was led to the consideration of logical, economic and ethical facts. If that were true, with the exception of his theory of æsthetics, practically the whole of his philosophy would be opened to the reproach that he levelled against the greatest part of the German æsthetic theories of the nineteenth century: "of not being derived from spontaneous and direct researches, but rather from the need of filling a compartment in a philosophical system." [2] A good many among Croce's critics have been the victims of such a misconception of the actual genesis of his thought; and have discounted the importance of any but his æsthetic theories, considering all the rest as a kind of philosophical by-product, with the result that they have not been able properly to understand even that part of his work in which they were interested. The typical example is given by those moralistic critics of his æsthetics, who would have been spared many mistakes and inanities, if they had thought Croce's ethics and logic worth a little consideration. They would then have realized that their criticisms had been anticipated and criti-

[1] *Contributo*, pp. 55–56.   [2] *Primi Saggi*, p. 163.

cized long before they had been uttered. But **perhaps** it is asking too much of the average student
of literature, once he has made the effort to think
about the problems of art, that he should also try
to turn the light of his reason on the obscure prompt-
ings of his moral consciousness; a suggestion which
in many cases would be violently rejected as the
height of immorality.

We shall soon see from which source Croce derived
his interest in economic problems and in the history
of the practical activities of man. Of the perma-
nence of those moral preoccupations which had been
his constant companions since his adolescence, we
find the traces in his autobiographical notes. In **De
Sanctis**, whose *History of Italian Literature* is as
much a moral as an æsthetic history of the Italian
people, he had the model of "a sound and simple
morality, austere without exaggerations, and high
without fanaticisms." [1]   But the same difficulties
which prevented him from fully understanding **De**
Sanctis' æsthetic principles, and from using them
as a vivifying element in his literary work, made
him also for a long time accept an inferior moral conception, that of **Herbart's** realism, "in which the
moral ideal was energetically asserted, but as a thing
of another world, as having man under itself as
brute matter, on which its stamp, more or less
marked, might or might not be impressed." That is,
he saw the moral ideal in relation to the actual life

[1] *Contributo,* p. 58.

of man, in a position similar to that which concepts and ideals had for him in relation to reality as a whole: his moral abstractism and rigorism was the counterpart of his logic. "But that rigorism and abstractism was the way that I had necessarily to follow in order to understand the moral concreteness, and to lift it to the plane of a philosophical theory." "And that rigorism, which was at the same time a love for sharp distinctions, while it saved me from associationism and positivism and evolutionism, put me on my guard against, and hindered me from falling into the errors of that now naturalistic, now mystic, Hegelianism, which through a hasty and often mythological dialectic, obliterated or weakened the distinctions which are the life of the dialectic process." [1] What Croce lacked, in ethics as well as in æsthetics, was a new logic or theory of knowledge, which would allow him to grasp the concept or the ideal, that is the universal, in the concrete spiritual activity, that is in the particular and individual. Meanwhile, his own dealing with abstract concepts, with purely formal universals, was to be, in relation to the further developments of his logic, what his early literary work, of a purely erudite character, had been in relation to his meditations on art and history: that personal experience, of difficulties and errors, without which no truth can ever be reached.

On the whole, Croce's position at that time was, as he himself defined it many years later, a Platonic-

---

[1] *Contributo*, pp. 59-60.

Scholastic-Herbartian one; one that, in the moral
field, had at least the advantage of being "invulner-
able to the subtle menace of sensualism and decadentism," [1] in the European life and thought of the
nineties, the acme of spiritual distinction—an illusory
reaction to and escape from the prevailing positivism
and determinism, of which in reality they were but
thinly disguised variations.   Croce "never lost,
even for an instant, the power of discerning sensual
refinement from spiritual finesse, erotic flights from
moral elevation, false heroism from sheer duty." [2]
Here lies the fundamental difference, "of spiritual
race," between him and his most illustrious contemporary, Gabriele d'Annunzio, with whom he has
more than once been coupled by superficial critics.
The character of their respective influence on the
younger Italian generations, of D'Annunzio between
1890 and 1900, and of Croce between 1900 and 1910,
is more than sufficient evidence on this point.

It is something of a surprise to find that he had
learnt practically nothing from his uncle Bertrando
Spaventa, who had been the most powerful representative of the Hegelian tradition in Italy.   The central problem of Spaventa's speculation had been
that of the relations between knowing and being,
of transcendence and immanence; and although it
was only through a solution of this problem that
Croce could hope for progress in any of his particular
philosophical researches, yet he could take no interest

[1] *Contributo*, p. 60.   [2] *Contributo*, p. 61.

in it when its discussion was carried on independently of those problems of art, of moral life, of law and history, towards which his attention was naturally drawn. Croce himself explains this lack of interest as due to his "unconscious immanentism": "as I met with no difficulty in conceiving the relation between thinking and being; if I had any difficulty, it was rather in conceiving a being severed from thought, or a thought severed from being." [1] But in this case he is probably seeing himself in the light of his later experience: that difficulty did exist, and is the fundamental difficulty of his early speculation. Only, he could not solve it by Spaventa's methods, which were those of a rigorous and formal logician, of a philosopher with a theological background, but only through the elaboration of the materials of his own particular moral and intellectual experience. At a later stage, and when he had already independently arrived at a position much more similar to that of Spaventa, than he would ever have thought possible for him, the influence, if not of Spaventa himself, at least of that attitude towards philosophy which had been his, came back to him through his friend Giovanni Gentile, whose mental temperament was much more akin to that of the old Neapolitan thinker, than Croce's ever was. Croce's idealism (or Hegelianism) was at this time limited to what he had unconsciously absorbed through De Sanctis' conception of art; but his theory of knowledge, not yet

[1] *Contributo*, p. 63.

logically unfolded, was still oscillating between **in-tellectualism** and naturalism. He was decidedly anti-Hegelian, on the other hand, in his theory of history and in **his** general **concep**tion **of** the world.

III. HISTORY AND ECONOMICS

In April, 1895, his old professor at the University of Rome, Antonio Labriola, sent to Croce an essay on the *Communist Manifesto,* in which he submitted to a critical examination the materialistic conception of history elaborated during the fifty preceding years by Karl Marx and Friedrich Engels. Labriola had been probably the first professor in a European University to take Historical Materialism as a subject for his academic lectures, his first course on Marxism having been delivered in 1889. But Croce, who had given all his thoughts first to his literary work, and then to his meditations on art and criticism, had not been as yet able to perceive the bearing of the new problems discussed by his master on that problem of the nature of history which had been the subject of his first philosophical essay, and was to be the centre of his later speculations. Labriola's little book came to him at a moment when he had reached an impasse in the course of his research, and it opened to him an entirely new field of investigations, it afforded him an escape towards

71

studies and meditations, at first apparently un-related to his former ones, but the results of which were destined to react vigorously on them. He plunged with youthful enthusiasm into the literature not of Marxism and historical materialism only, but of Economics in general. In the five following years, while he continued with unremitting energy his literary labours, now more clearly directed towards an understanding of the historical problems of Æsthetics, and a clarification of the concepts of a philosophical science of Æsthetics, he published a series of critical essays on *Materialismo storico ed economia marxistica*, intended at the same time as a defence and a rectification of Marx's doctrines.

We shall consider this phase of Croce's work from two distinct points of view—as a new individual experience, and as a stage in the development of his philosophy. For the first of them, we shall again leave the word to Croce himself: "That inter-course with the literature of Marxism, and the eagerness with which for some time I followed the socialistic press of Germany and Italy, stirred my whole being, and for the first time awakened in me a feeling of political enthusiasm, yielding a strange taste of newness to me: I was like a man who having fallen in love for the first time when no longer young, should observe in himself the mysterious process of the new passion. At that fire I burnt also my ab-stract moralism, and I learnt that the course of history has a right to drag and to crush the individual.

As I had not been disposed in my family circle to any fanaticism, and not even to a liking for the current and conventional liberalism of Italian politics . . . it seemed to me to breathe faith and hope in the vision of the rebirth of mankind redeemed by labour and in labour." [1] This political enthusiasm did not last very long: it disappeared when that which was Croce's true nature, not practical but essentially theoretical, reasserted itself, by reducing this new experience into new conceptual forms; but without it, the whole of his philosophy of the practical activity would forever have been like a theory of vision in the mind of a blind man, or a theory of love in that of a keeper of the harem. Art, thought, mortality, had already appeared to him as aspects of his own life; to these, a new element was added now, not as a mere object of thought, but as a passionate and concrete experience.

The interpretation of the doctrine of historical materialism presented a number of difficulties deriving partly from the form in which the doctrine itself had originally appeared—not as a coherent theory, but as a series of pronouncements and observations scattered in a variety of writings, composed at a distance of years, and the aim of which was rather political and polemical than scientific; and partly from its association with remnants of old metaphysics, both in its originators and in their followers. In Marx and Engels, as well as practically in the

[1] *Contributo*, pp. 36–37.

whole literature of Marxism, the emphasis being
laid on the substantive rather than on the adjective,
historical materialism implied the adhesion to that
metaphysical materialism which was one of the
children of Hegelian metaphysics. What had been
the Idea for Hegel, was the Economy of the new
metaphysicians: the only reality, working beneath
the surface of human consciousness, as an under-
structure beneath a merely apparent and illusory
superstructure. Given this conception, it is easy to
understand why historical materialism appealed
so strongly to positivists and evolutionists, who concealed a similar kind of metaphysics under their
proclaimed contempt for philosophy. The old
philosophies of history had attempted to reduce the
sequence of history to a scheme of concepts, starting with God, or Providence, or the Hegelian
Idea: the new unconscious metaphysicians substituted for the old concepts that of Economy, or of
Matter, or of Development and Evolution, from
which all the particular historical determinations
could be deduced with not less certainty than from
the old metaphysical entities. And from their
predecessors they also borrowed those teleological
tendencies which are implicit in all metaphysics,
attributing a will and an end to their new God, be
it called Progress or Matter, and trying to deduce
the future course of history from the dialectic of
the past. Hence the growth of a vast literature
inquiring into the development of abstract sociological

schemes or of economic forms reduced to characteristics of economic epochs, forcing the concrete materials of history into rigid conceptual frames; hence
the naïve faith in the deduction of social predeter-
minations, of which the most striking was the asserted necessity of the advent of socialism as the
only logical outcome of capitalist society.

Croce, pursuing the analysis initiated by Labriola,
began by dissociating what seemed to him to be the
vital element in historical materialism, from any
intrusion of either Hegelian or positivistic metaphysics. His criticism of historical materialism as
a philosophy of history and, generally, of the possibility of constructing any philosophy of history,
is the first resolute step towards an antimetaphysical
conception of philosophy. Whether by metaphysics
is meant the knowledge of another world of real
essences, of things in themselves, beyond the objects
of our immediate experience, or the creation of abstract concepts duplicating and falsifying the complex world of life, the whole trend of Croce's thought
will henceforward oppose any claim on the part of
these spurious philosophies, mythological or pseudo-
scientific, to furnish an adequate interpretation of
reality. Vico's metaphysics of human ideas, which
is no metaphysics at all, because it does not postulate
the existence of any reality beyond that of the spirit
of man, will more and more become the model of
Croce's own philosophy. That immanentism which
he considers as one of the spontaneous attitudes

of his mind slowly extricates itself from the ruins of his own transcendental logic, and shows itself impervious to the allurements of both Platonism and Positivism, of the ancient and the new myth.

Purged of its unessential philosophical associations, historical materialism (or, more precisely, the economic interpretation of history) appeared to Croce as nothing more than a new canon or criterion of historical interpretation, fixing the attention of the historian on a mass of new data, the importance of which had not been recognized before. It was neither a new philosophy nor a new method: it could not be legitimately employed to draw con-clusions on the relations between economic facts and the other facts of history, nor to reduce history itself to the operation of a few abstract laws. It was a tendency of historical thought, coinciding with the manifestation of certain objective con-ditions of society (the industrial revolution) and their reflexes in political thought, by which the economic element in social facts acquired a stronger relief than it had ever had in the consciousness of man. And it seemed to point, both for the historian and for the philosopher, towards the existence of a fundamental principle or form of human activity— economic activity, about the nature of which, and its relation with æsthetic, logic, and moral activity, very little had been thought and written, besides what is contained in the introductions to all classical manuals of political economy. While still insisting

that history is art, that is, the representation of
individual happenings, Croce was thus implicitly
brought to admit of the importance of philosophy,
that is, of the study of the fundamental forms or
categories of human activity, for the historian. His
conception of history was undergoing a transformation in a direction similar to that towards which
his conception of philosophy was moving.

When he passed from the consideration of the
general theory to the examination of more technical
aspects of Marx's doctrines, the first difficulty which
presented itself to him was that of the relations
between Marxian economics and pure economics,
or general economic science. The society whose
economic life Marx had studied in *Das Kapital*, was
neither human society in general, nor any particular
historical society, but a purely ideal and formal
society deduced from a proposition assumed outside the fields of pure economics: that of the equivalence of value and labour. Starting from this
postulate, Marx had proceeded to inquire into those
processes of differentiation between the assumed
standard and the actual prices of commodities in a
capitalist society, by which labour itself acquires a
price and becomes a commodity. It was a method
of scientific analysis consisting in regarding a phenomenon not as it actually exists, but as it would be
if one of its factors were altered, and in comparing
the hypothetical with the real phenomenon, conceiving of the first as diverging from the second

which is postulated as fundamental, or the second as diverging from the first, which is postulated in the same manner. It is only when the whole of Marxian economics is considered as the application of such a method, that the concepts of labour-value and of surplus-value acquire a definite and precise meaning: the description of economic society as a pure working society (producing no goods which cannot be increased by labour) must then be interpreted as a concept of difference, or an instrument of elliptical comparison, as against the descriptions of actual economic society given by pure economics. Its positive value, not as an abstract hypothesis, but as a means of knowledge, depends on the fact that such a society does actually coincide with certain aspects of historical capitalist society; that the equivalence of labour and value is not a purely imaginary fact, but a fact among other facts, empirically opposed, limited, and distorted by other facts. Having assumed this equivalence as a test for the study of the social problem of labour, Marx's object was to show the special way in which this problem is solved in a capitalist society. And this was the real justification for his employment of the hypothetical method.

It is clear that Croce was infinitely more interested in what Marx had actually accomplished, than in what he had intended to do. In Marx's own mind, the analysis of the conditions of capitalist society led inevitably to the conclusion that a passage from capitalism to socialism was predetermined by the structure of capitalist society itself. It is well known that the prevision assumed what claimed to be a strictly scientific character in the formulation of the law of the fall in the rate of profits: the gradual decrease of surplus-values accompanying the increase in technical improvements, and automatically reestablishing the equivalence of labour and value. Croce offered a very convincing criticism of this law on Marx's own grounds, by showing that it rested on a confusion between technical and economic facts, thus affording a remarkable example of Marx's uncertainty of his own method. It was clear that in this particular case Marx had been carried away by his desire to reduce the metaphysical implications of his economic sociology to the status of an historical law. And Croce's criticism was evidently intended both to deprive Marx's historical determinism of one of its most powerful instruments, and to confirm his own view of the method which gave validity and importance to such economic speculations as Marx's were.

Marxian economics stood thus interpreted as comparative sociological economics, and by the definition Croce also defined the scope of sociological science, and the nature of the logical processes which it could legitimately employ. It was a considerable advance in the study of scientific concepts, as distinct from purely speculative concepts. But he still believed at the time, misled by the economists' discussions on

the nature of the economic principle, that pure economics and the philosophy of economics practically
coincided; and as he had maintained the legitimacy
of Marx's method against the criticisms of the pure,
or scientific, economists, he defended pure economics
against Marx and his school, as the general science
of the economic datum. But he was soon to understand that his own point of view and that of the pure
economists were widely divergent, and that the
methods of pure economics are in fact scientific and
not philosophical. In later years, when he came to
regard the science of economics as an empirical and
mathematical science, Marxian economics appeared to
him merely as a special branch of economic casuistry,
employing methods fundamentally identical with
those of pure economics: a relationship which could
be illustrated by a comparison with the parallel of
non-Euclidean and classical geometry. Although he
did not reach this final position at the time, there is
no doubt that his experience of the actual scientific
processes of economics freed him from his allegiance
to Herbartian logic, in which science and philosophy
were still formally undifferentiated, and led him gradually to the distinction between the scientific and the
speculative concept, of which the relation established
between Marxian and pure economics is a tentative
prefiguration.

But the most essential gain of his economic studies
was in the direction of the affirmation of the merely
practical, or economic, principle, as one of the irre-

ducible forms of human activity, raising the concept of the Useful to the same level (logically speaking) at which those of the Beautiful, the True, and the Good had been kept by the whole European philosophical tradition since Plato. He was here actually elaborating not a scientific, but a speculative concept, though his approach to it was always by means of the discussion of particular problems, the solution of which implied a definite view of the relations between the economic principle on one side, and respectively on the other side, the intellectual and the moral principle.

As regards the possibility of inferring practical programmes from scientific principles, he objected that neither the desirable nor the practicable are science. Science may be a legitimate means of simplifying problems, making it possible to distinguish in them what can be scientifically ascertained from what can only be partially known; in the case of the Marxian law of the fall in the rate of profits, for instance, if such a law were proved to be scientifically correct, it could be said, under certain conditions that the end of capitalist society was a scientific certainty, though it would remain doubtful what would follow it. But logic is not life, and the appraisement of social programmes is a matter of empirical observations and of practical convictions. The unconquerable indetermination of social facts brings forth that element of daring in the actions of practical men, which is to will what inspiration is to expression, insight to intellect, in the poet and in the scientist.

Socialism could not be called a scientific programme, except in a limited and metaphorical sense, which was not a criticism of socialism itself, but of the bad logic of certain Socialists: the Marxian programme as such, Croce recognized as one of the noblest and boldest, and also one of those which obtain the greatest support from the objective conditions of existing society. Having already denied the dependence of intellectual truth on economic fact, by criticising the metaphysics of historical materialism, he thus asserted now the autonomy of the economic from the logical principle.

On the other hand, he destroyed the legend of the intrinsic immorality of Marxism, which was due to Marx's repeated assertions that the social question is not a moral question, and to his sharp criticisms of class ideals and hypocrisies. He pointed to the moral interest which had guided Marx's political activity, and which could even be said to have prompted the choice of the fundamental hypotheses of his economics. What Marx had called the impotence of morality was the futile attempt at apportioning praise or blame for the natural conditions of the social order. It is only when such conditions are no longer conceived as necessary for the social order in general, but only for a stage in its history, and when new conditions appear that make it possible to destroy them, that moral condemnation is justified and effective: to use another of Marx's phrases, morality condemns what history has already condemned. This is as much as saying that the only real moral problems, as all other problems of human life, are those that present themselves under given historical circumstances, at a given time; concrete, not abstract; and that moral judgments apply not to facts or conditions, but to actions. The passage from such a concrete, or historical, view of morality, to a doctrine of moral relativity is a very easy one, but Marx's own views on this point, which he never deliberately expounded, are irrelevant to the substance of his doctrine. For his own part, Croce reasserted the value of Kantian ethics, and the absoluteness of the moral ideal, as an ideal which is not above and outside the spirit of man, but rather one of its intrinsic forms or categories. And Marx's conclusions in regard to the function of morality in the social movement, and to the method for the education of the proletariat, though clashing with current prejudices, contain no contradiction of general ethical principles. But Marx's interest was not essentially an ethical one: the moralistic criticisms of Marx were similar to the puritanic criticisms of Machiavelli, and resolved themselves into a charge that neither the one nor the other had treated problems totally different from those which they had actually attempted to clarify. While vindicating the importance of Machiavelli in the history of the study of the economic activity of man, Croce called Marx himself the Machiavelli of the labour movement, implicitly suggesting a similarity of both object and method between *Il Principe* and *Das Kapital*, which is singularly illuminating.

The last essays of the book on *Materialismo Storico* are two letters to Professor Pareto "On the Economic Principle," written in 1900; but with these we reach a time when Croce's thought was already organizing itself in the system of the philosophy of mind. In them we find a sketch of the system in the form in which it appeared in the first edition of the *Estetica:* that is, we already decidedly enter into the maturer phase of Croce's thought. We must here pause on the threshold, and looking back on the years of Croce's special interest in economic problems, sum up the new elements that the study of these problems adds to his intellectual physiognomy: a more deliberately antimetaphysical attitude, a growing consciousness of the complexity of history and of the concreteness of moral life, a realization of the function of the economic activity, a progress in the analysis of scientific concepts, and therefore in the foundations of his logic—but, most important of all, a continued practice of philosophical thought under the shape of historical methodology. Apart from their interest as documents of the growth of his philosophy, Croce's studies have also a place in the history of social and economic thought, side by side with those of Labriola and of Georges Sorel, as a significant episode in that Latin crisis of Marxism, the ultimate outcome of which are the theories of French and Italian Syndicalism.

PART SECOND
THE PHILOSOPHY OF MIND
(1900–1910)

I. THE GROWTH OF THE SYSTEM

THE salient feature of Croce's mind, fully displaying itself in the maturity of his work, is a power to follow different lines of thought and research, without either confusing the issues or losing sight of the deep underlying connections. For the average scholar, an incursion into alien ground will generally mark the abandonment of his former interests; or, in the best hypothesis, the creation of a new mental personality coexisting with the original one, but neither reacting on it nor being influenced by it. The reason is obvious: the substance of each personality is a cross-section of the body of one discipline, which in its actual history, in its methods, associations and sphere of interest, touches the other one at very few points only, if at any at all. The establishment of new relations between the two requires a new personal elaboration, a complete individual mastery of the materials and methods of each discipline. We are hardly aware of the independence gained by even very closely related fields of research through the specialistic treatment of the last century: how each of them has developed, so to speak, a language of its own, which has its foundation in the peculiar, and inevitable, terminology, but extends far beyond it into the logical structure of the specialist mind. We have more or less consciously built up a world (that is, an implicit conception of the world, a naïve philosophy) for the economist, one for the biologist, one for the mathematician, one for the student of literature, and so on. The scholar with the dual personality lives alternatively in separate and self-contained worlds; but to melt the two images into a single one, is far beyond his power. In other cases, he will relate all the experiences legitimately belonging to one special world, to another one, probably to the one with which he was first acquainted; but then we have those awkward hybrids, the economics of the literary man, or the literature of the biologist, or the biology of the economist; and the confusion is so apparent that it generally reflects itself in the very quality of the terminology employed.

It was against this kind of confusion, against the transference of the concepts of one science into another, which was the favourite device of positivism, that Croce continually reacted in his criticism of contemporary thought. He instinctively knew the value of distinctions, and also the value of unity; but he would never pay for unity at the expense of the fine, precise, necessary distinctions. This explains why for a certain number of years he may have appeared as a man occupied in the pursuit of two quite different and unconnected lines of research:

his literary friends used to look on his economic studies with wonder and distrust, as on a strange whim and a total waste of time, while the economists more or less resented the intrusion of the outsider. But it explains also why, when he finally attempted to give shape to the conclusions he had reached in regard to one particular group of problems, his grasp of the essential unity and his power to build an inclusive and unspecialized conception of reality, were made visible at once. There was no special problem of thought which could be treated apart from an either implicit or explicit view of the whole of reality: there was no solution of any particular problem which would not affect, and in turn be affected by, the solution of every other problem. Or, to say the same thing in different words, philosophy was a system, not in the sense that a rigid logical scheme could once and forever fit the ever moving stream of reality, but because it is impossible to think the distinctions without the unity, or the unity without the distinctions. That which appears to us, psychologically, as the main characteristic of Croce's mind, transforms itself into the intrinsic logic of his system, in which the principles of unity and of distinction are, as we shall see, fundamental.

In the year 1899 Croce had been compelled to spend a good part of his time in a more or less practical activity in connection with the Centenary of the Neapolitan Republic of 1799, and it was only towards the end of that year that he could dedicate himself entirely to the work he had constantly had in mind since the publication of his essays on literary criticism: the exposition of his concept of art in the fulness of its relations and determinations. It will be well to let Croce himself give us an account of that decisive moment, of the ripening and gathering of his various speculations into their first coherent and systematic expression. "When I started my work, and began to collect my scattered thoughts, I found myself extremely ignorant: the gaps multiplied themselves in my sight; those same things that I thought I held well in my grasp wavered and became confused; unsuspected questions came forward asking for an answer; and during five months I read almost nothing, walked for hours and hours, spent half days and whole days lying on a couch, searching assiduously within myself, and putting down on paper notes and thoughts, each of which was a criticism of the other. This torment grew much worse, when in November I tried to set forth in a concise memoir the fundamental theses of Æsthetics, because, ten times at least, having carried my work up to a certain point, I became aware of the necessity of taking a step which was not justified logically, and I started all over again in order to discover in the beginnings the obscurity or error which had brought me to that quandary; and, having rectified the error, again went my way, and a little further I again stumbled into a similar difficulty. Only after six or seven more months was I able to send to the press that memoir in the form in which it has been printed under the title *Tesi fondamentali di un' Estetica come scienza dell' espressione e linguistica generale;* arid and abstruse, but from which, once I had finished it, I came out not only quite oriented in regard to the problems of the mind, but also with an awakened and sure understanding of almost all the principal problems about which classical philosophers have toiled: an understanding which cannot be acquired by merely reading their books, but only by repeating within oneself, under the stimulus of life, their mental drama." [1]

We are so used to see the intellectual worker surrounded and propped up by libraries, laboratories, files, and statistics, that the sight of a man abandoning his books, giving himself up to what by all material standards must be classed as a state of idleness, in order to withdraw into the intimacy of his own consciousness, there to find an answer to the problems of reality, cannot but strike us as incongruous and anachronistic. If we were frank about ourselves, we should confess that our unbounded confidence in the purely material helps is merely a mask for our deep-rooted scepticism, for our absolute lack of confidence in the power of reason. What we cannot hope to attain through our individual effort, we expect as the product of a great machine of thought, in which man enters as a little wheel, accomplishing a given function, as mechanical and

[1] *Contributo*, pp. 40-41.

impersonal as the rest of the machine. We strive for objectivity, and believe in the automatic fabrication of truth. Through a false analogy with the methods of the natural sciences, imperfectly understood, and assimilated to those of industrial production, we call this process scientific, and we pretend to despise what we fear, the testimony of our consciousness and the hardships of personal thought. Reason, the human reason, the ultimate source of all knowledge, we pay lip homage to, but really put in the same category as the obscure intuition of the mystic. Outside our mechanical objectivity, we seem unable to see anything but an arbitrary subjectivism, a capricious and empirical individuality.

But however incongruous and anachronistic it may appear to us, there is little doubt that this method is the only philosophical method, the method of philosophy in all times. Croce's originality consists merely in having reasserted its validity in such sharp contrast to all the tendencies of the age, and to have shown that true objectivity belongs only to the truth we discover within ourselves, when the eye of our mind is not turned on the transient spectacle of our superficial life, but is reaching under it for that universal consciousness which is the foundation of the individual one. There is no scholar who is as exacting and punctilious as Croce in the choice and elaboration of his material— as conscious of the need of thoroughness and precision—as impatient of any form of improvisation;

but he never forgets that the end of all his labours is merely that of *knowing himself*, in the spirit of the ancient oracle, by acquiring a direct, intimate experience of the processes through which a mind of to-day has come to be what is truly is; of making his own individual consciousness partake more and more of that universality which alone is true consciousness, by liberating itself from all casual determinations, and becoming historically acquainted with itself. It is easy to see how in such a general attitude the road to philosophy is also the road to history; and how both in philosophy and in history the final test must be not that of the dead material, but of the living spirit.

The employment of such a method leads to two consequences: the first, that a philosophy thus conceived will be a philosophy of the human spirit—*Filosofia dello Spirito*—or, as we, following the habits of English-speaking philosophers, shall tentatively call it, a philosophy of mind; the second, that the universality which the individual spirit discovers within itself, not being a static, immovable universality, but merely the form of its ever-changing, historical actuality, philosophy itself will be a continuous progress, and at no particular moment will it be possible to define the thought of the philosopher as a completed system. As we cannot, however, in the small compass of this book, minutely follow all the successive modifications and accretions of Croce's thought, we shall speak of the ten years between 1900 and 1910 as of the period in which the system of the philosophy of mind was developed and determined, and we shall attempt in the following chapters to give a general view of the system itself as it might have appeared in 1910 to a conscientious student of all the works of Croce published during that interval of time.

The *Tesi* contained already the substance of the *Estetica come scienza dell' espressione e linguistica generale* which was completed in 1901 and published in 1902, and with which Croce definitely took his place in modern philosophy. The book is divided in two parts, the exposition of the theory and the history of the doctrine. But the two parts are very closely related to each other, as the exposition already criticises all the possible aspects of æsthetic theory, and the history merely disposes the same criticisms in a chronological order, and labels each of them with a name. This plan, with slight alterations, is that of the successive volumes of the *Filosofia dello Spirito:* to the reader who is already acquainted with the history of philosophy, the historical character of the purely theoretical exposition is readily apparent.

Soon after the publication of the *Estetica*, Croce began to consider his book merely as a programme and a sketch which needed filling in with further developments,—with the investigation of the other forms of human activity, which had been merely postulated in the study of the æsthetic activity; and with a wide cultural work, to be carried on especially by means of a review, through which his ideas should be tested in immediate and constant relation with the problems of contemporary Italian and European thought. The enormous activity of the following years falls easily into this rough division. On one hand we have the completion of the *Filosofia dello Spirito*, with the *Logica come scienza del concetto puro*, the first edition of which appeared in 1905 (*Lineamenti di una Logica*, etc.), and the second, deeply modified by his meditations on the practical activity, in 1909, with the *Filosofia della Pratica: Economica ed Etica*, written in 1908, but of which some parts had already been given in 1907 in the memoir *Riduzione della filosofia del diritto alla filosofia dell' economia;* and with the new and fuller formulation of his Æsthetics in a paper read to the International Congress of Philosophy in Heidelberg in 1908, on *L'intuizione pura e il carattere lirico dell' arte.* To these must be added the two monographs on *Hegel* (1906) and *Vico* (1910), which are at the same time an exposition of their philosophies and a restatement of Croce's own main positions, in so far as they coincided with those elements of truth which he still recognized as living in their thought.

On the other hand we have the publication of a bi-monthly review, *La Critica*, the first number of which appeared in January, 1903, and which is still being published. *La Critica* announced itself as a review of literature, history and philosophy, but it differed from all other publications in the same fields in two

main features: the first, that the number of its con-
tributors was practically limited to two, Croce himself, and his friend Giovanni Gentile, with whom he
had first been brought in contact through their common interest in Marxian studies, and who followed
for some years at least a line of thought which
touched his own at many points; the second, that it
imposed upon itself a very definite programme of
work, each number containing an essay, or part of an
essay, by Croce on some Italian writter of the preceding half-century, and one by Gentile on the
Italian philosophers of the same period, besides a
number of reviews of new Italian and foreign books,
and notes and comments on contemporary questions
of culture and moral life. In his own main work for
the *Critica*, Croce was at the same time aiming at
giving concrete examples of the application of
æsthetic theory in the domain of literary criticism,
and at clearing the ground for the work of the new
generation, through an appraisement of the literary
values of the preceding one. The general temper of
the review is clearly expressed in the following words
from the already so often quoted autobiographical
notes: "The ideal which I cherished was drawn not
from my own personality, but from my varied experience, because, having lived sufficiently in the
academic world to know both its virtues and its
faults, and having at the same time preserved a
feeling of real life, and of literature and science as
being born from it and renovating themselves in it,

I addressed my censures and my polemics on one hand against dilettanti and unmethodical workers, on the other against the academicians resting in their prejudices and idling with the externals of art and science." [1]

The greatest part of the writings contributed by Croce to the *Critica* during these years were later collected in volumes, of which however only the *Problemi d'Estetica* (1910), containing, besides the Heidelberg lecture, a large number of essays both on the theory and history of Æsthetics, appeared before the end of the period we are now considering. To intensify the action of both his books and his review, he initiated in 1906, in connection with the publisher Laterza of Bari, the publication of a series of *Classici della filosofia moderna*, in which he published his own translation of Hegel's *Encyclopedia;* and in 1909, of the collection *Scrittori d' Italia*, which is in the way to becoming the standard *corpus* of Italian Literature. He took also a leading part in the editing of the same publisher's *Biblioteca di cultura moderna*, which was enriched through his care and advice with reprints of rare works of southern Italian writers of the Risorgimento and of the early years of the Unity, and with translations of books representative of foreign contemporary thought.

If we add to all this, a number of scattered essays and monographs, editions of texts and documents, and bibliographies, and the generous coöperation,

[1] *Contributo*, p. 48.

extending from the friendly discussion of plans and ideas to the humble reading of proofs, with a host of friends and disciples, we have a fairly complete idea of the significance of Croce in the cultural life of young Italy. He very rapidly became something like an institution; he was hailed as the master and spiritual guide of the new generation. His work and his example, the clarity of his thought and the rhythm of his steady, harmonious, powerful activity, were an element not of the limited life of the intellectual laboratory only, but of the spiritual life of the nation.

II. INTUITION AND EXPRESSION [1]

The four grades of spiritual activity—Intuition and conceptual knowledge—The intuitive consciousness—The limits of intuitive knowledge—Identifications of intuition and expression—Art as expression:
content and form—Language as expression; the reality of words—
Croce's use of the word intuition—The lyrical character of the pure
intuition.

THE whole cycle of the philosophy of mind exhausts itself in the study of the four fundamental
forms of human activity, the concepts of which we
have seen slowly developing through the mazes
of Croce's early speculations: the æsthetic, the
logic, the economic and the ethic; of the distinction
and the unity of æsthetic and logic in the theoretical
activity, or knowledge, and of economic and ethic
in the practical activity, or action; and finally of the
relations between the theoretical and the practical,
or knowledge and action. This may be said to be
the positive aspect of Croce's philosophy: the negative aspect consists in the criticism and exclusion
of any other form of activity from the system of
the human spirit, and of that which is not the spirit,
or nature, from the system of reality.

[1] This chapter and the following two are founded especially on the
Estetica, pp. 1–171; the essay on *L'intuizione pura e il carattere lirico dell'*
arte, in *Problemi*, pp. 1–30; and the *Breviario*, in *Nuovi Saggi*, pp. 1–91.

To the four forms or grades of spiritual activity, correspond four philosophical sciences: Æsthetics, Logic, Economics, and Ethics. Each of them can be said to be the *organum* of the particular form of activity which it studies; the affirmation of that sphere of consciousness which is proper to it, and of its relations to the other forms. Each of them is therefore related to the others in the same way as the various forms of activity are related to each other. They might be defined as the projection on the plane of logic of the whole system of human activity, that is, of the whole of reality. They derive their intrinsic validity from this perfect coincidence of their several objects with the only conceivable aspects of reality.

We shall in this and in the following chapters attempt to fill in with the strictly necessary detail this very ample frame. But we can already point to the idealistic character of such a philosophy resulting from its method, which is that of the testimony of consciousness, as opposed to the naturalistic or psychologic method of indirect observation; from its object, which is the human spirit or mind in the fulness of its determinations; and from the exclusion of any aspect of reality which is not immanent in consciousness, that is, both of the naturally and the supernaturally transcendent. As against another kind of idealism, of which the typical example is Platonic transcendentalism, Croce's idealism is realistic and immanentistic: the task of the philosophy of mind is to discover the immanent logic of reality.   But against current realism, which considers mind as the mere spectator and observer of external or natural reality, it asserts the identity of reality and consciousness, which is the basic position of all idealism.

There are two forms of knowledge: intuitive (or æsthetic) and conceptual (or logical).   Intuition is the knowledge of the individual or particular; the concept is the knowledge of the universal.   This distinction, as we have already seen, corresponds roughly to the old classical distinction of *mythos* and *logos*, to Vico's definitions of poetry and metaphysics, and to the new meaning given by Baumgarten to the old antithesis of *aisthēta* and *noēta*. Let us quote Vico again: "Men first feel without perceiving, then they perceive and are perturbed and moved; finally they reflect with pure mind." Here we have three successive grades, of which the first is mere sensation, the lower limit of mental activity; the second is intuition; the third, concept. For Vico, the second grade is identical with Poetry, and the science of this form of knowledge, which we call Æsthetics, he called Poetic Logic, the science of poetry as "the first operation of the human mind."   Vico's discovery consists in this definition of Poetry (and Art), not as a casual, capricious, lateral form of spiritual activity, but as the first and necessary grade of knowledge, as an essential function of the mind.   But Vico's thought was clothed in what we might well call a mythological form: the various grades of spiritual activity were presented by him as successive stages or epochs in the history of mankind; and the inter-relation of the various grades, as the actual law of the development of human society. Croce unravelled Vico's philosophy, or ideal history, history of the mind, from Vico's concrete, sociological history, and the result was this new Æsthetics which is at the same time a science of the first grade of knowledge, and of art and language.

Of the reality of intuitive, as distinct from reflected knowledge, we have constant evidence in our immediate experience. If I examine my own consciousness, at any particular moment, I find it crowded with *things I know*, as, now, this room in which I am writing, the piano that is open before me, the flowers in a little basket, blue fragments of sky and green branches washed by the recent rain swaying in the clear sunlight, the shrill voice of a child from the road, the light steps of a girl moving about the house. I am not conscious of all these intuitions at once: I write, and I distinctly *know* this white paper only, and the black signs I am tracing, the pen guided by my hand, and the edges of a few books on my table: all the rest has faded away into a blurred, confused intuition, the intuition of an atmosphere, composed of mere shreds and shadows of the colours and sounds of which I was so distinctly conscious but one minute ago. But now I put down my pen again, and I look at the piano; and I let my mind wander away, from what I see to what I remember or imagine: the fair-headed figure playing this morning Franck's Prelude, Choral and Fugue, the rapid and sure movements of the fingers on the white and black keys, a vague image of the solemn and passionate music, memories of distant days, a sudden rush of obscure fantasies, evoked by the actual playing, and still lingering in the recesses of my mind, returning now with a fragment of a melody, with a succession of triumphant chords. And again, I look beyond the window, and the little square of green and blue expands itself into the vast valley beyond, screened from my view by these few trees clustering around the house, and yet mysteriously present to my inner eye: I see a little company of riders cantering along a shaded lane, coming out in an open meadow surrounded by low, thick-wooded hills; the sun sets in a pale purple sky, and I hear the tramping of the slow, heavy hoofs, as the horses find their way back through the woods, through a darkness much more opaque and solid than that of the remote twilight, still visible above the highest branches, animated by the first faint glittering of a star. And the woods are full of a myriad small breathing and stirring noises, of the sense of the deep surging inhuman life of trees and shrubs, of the penetrating scent of the rich damp earth, of decaying wood, of fallen leaves.

And now, I suddenly shut myself out of this world of perceptions and imaginations, or rather I keep them all before me, but not because of the immediate, individual interest I have in each of them. I try to extract the common, the universal element of which I suspect the existence not beyond but within them. I renounce all particular intuitions for the concept of intuition. I am no longer an image-making mind, no longer engaged in this elementary or "first" operation of the human mind, but I have passed on to a different, and manifestly a "secondary" plane of mental activity, since it would be impossible for me to root my thinking anywhere but on the soil of my intuitions.

What, then, is intuition? Clearly it is not the mere sensation, the formless matter which the mind cannot grasp in itself, as mere matter, but possesses only by imposing its form on it. Without matter no human knowledge or activity is possible, but matter is, within ourselves, the animal element, that which is brutal and impulsive, not the spiritual domain, which is humanity. Matter conquered by form gives place to the concrete form. Matter, or content, is what differentiates one intuition from another; the form is constant, and the form is the spiritual activity. In this way we set the lower limit of intuitive knowledge, and we recognize its characters of awareness and activity: an intuition is not that which presents itself to me, but that which I make my own, by giving form to it. It may be an actual perception, but the distinction between that which is real and that which is imaginary is not an intuitive, but a logical or intellectual one; the knowledge of things which I do not perceive, but only remember, or even only create with my imagination belongs to the same class, partakes of the same formal character. Space and time, which have more than once been considered as intuitions, are in reality categories of an intellectual order: they may be found in intuitions, as other intellectual elements are found, but as ingredients and not as necessary elements, *materialiter* and not *formaliter*. In relation to the usual psychological concepts of association and representation, it can be said that an intuition is an association, when by that word we mean an active mental synthesis, and not a mechanical juxtaposition of abstract sensations; and that it is a representation, not as a complex sensation, but as a spiritual elaboration of the sensation.

The upper limit of intuitive knowledge is given by reflected, or intellectual, or logical knowledge, or whatever we may call that which is no longer knowledge of the individual, of things, but of the universal, of relations among things, of concepts. Intuitive knowledge is independent of intellectual knowledge, as it is possible to form intuitions without forming concepts; in the examples which I have given in the preceding paragraph, practically all the intuitions are pure intuitions, in the

sense that they do not contain any logical ingredients. But even when such are found, they appear
as mere intuitions, and not as concepts: as, for instance, Hamlet's philosophy, which I do not read
as a help towards the understanding of metaphysical problems, but as a characterization of an im-
aginery individual. On the other hand, logical
knowledge is founded on intuitions, presupposes
the world of intuitions as its matter or content.
The relation between æsthetic and logical knowledge is one of grade or development: the former
stands by itself, rests directly on that which is not
yet spirit or form, is the first grade of spiritual or
human activity; the latter gives a further spiritual
elaboration to the intuitive material. This relationship, to which we shall return later, is the
typical process of Croce's own logic, the logic
of spiritual or mental grades, which he substitutes
throughout his system for the naturalistic or transcendental logic of his early masters.

A further step in the deduction of the concept
of intuitive or æsthetic knowledge, is made by
identifying intuition with expression. Given the
active and conscious character of intuition, we
are already prepared to admit that every true intuition is at the same time an expression; that
which cannot objectify itself into an expression is
nothing but mere sensation. The mind does not
actually intuit except by doing, forming, and expressing. We must not think only of verbal ex-

pressions: there are intuitions which cannot be expressed by words, but only by sounds or lines or colours. But in any case the two words are interchangeable: what really exists in our spirit is only what we can express. It is only when we can express ourselves, that we are conscious of actually possessing, that is, of having actually formed, our intuitions. It is impossible to distinguish the expression from the intuition because they are not two but one.

This identification runs counter to a number of very common and very dear delusions: we constantly imagine that the difference between ourselves and a great painter or a great poet does not consist in the power of seeing and feeling, but in a supposed gift of merely external expression; and again, we credit ourselves with a number of thoughts and images, which we might express if we only wished to. The easiest way to free ourselves of such delusions is to try to express whatever it seems to us that we possess: it becomes then apparent that our pictorial or poetical intuitions are really mere fragments, or echoes, of intuitions; are, in fact, not more than that which we succeed in expressing. It must however be borne in mind that we give here to the word expression a purely mental or spiritual significance: we mean by it the image that we form in our mind, and of which the painting or the poem, as objects, are the material extrinsications. It requires but little reflection to realize that there is

no painting or poem—there is no word that we utter
—unless it be a mere *flatus vocis*, which has not been
preceded in our mind by an internal image, which
is the true expression.

The reader will have remarked that, in order to
give examples of intuitive knowledge, we have now
had recourse to poetry and to painting. The fact
is that there is no difference between intuitive
knowledge, or expression, and art, except a purely
extensive and empirical one: that is, we call a poet
or an artist a man who possesses this expressive
power in a higher degree than the rest of mankind;
we call a poem or a work of art an expression which
is fuller, more complex, more elaborate, than those
which are the product of our common intuitive
activity, mere waves of the continuous stream of
spiritual life, in which they are constantly interrupted by and mixed with reflections and volitions,
with logical and practical facts. The difference
between the genius and the common man, in the
æsthetic as well as in the other spheres of human
activity, is a quantitative, not a qualitative one.
Art is not a peculiar spiritual function, and therefore a closed circle to which none but the elect are
admitted: the artist appeals to the intuitive man
in each of us, in a language of which every human
mind finds the key within itself.

The definition of art as expression emphasizes
the creative and formal character of art; and its
immediate consequence is the identification of form

and content, that is, the solution of one of the oldest and most confused of æsthetic problems. Art is form, not in the technical or formalistic sense, but in the meaning which we have given to the word when discussing the relation between sensation and intuition; and the content of a particular work of art cannot be abstracted from the work itself as something that existed before it, and to which a form has been added from outside. There is no content, in art, which is not the content of a particular form, that is, that which has ceased to exist as a possible content, and has transformed itself into a definite form. This conception of the relations of form and content implies also either a new interpretation, or the repudiation, of the theory of art as the imitation of nature, meaningless in a mechanical sense, true, and synonymous with the theory of intuition, in a creative and formative sense. Through the same critical process, all discussions of the relations between art and the senses appear as being founded on a confusion between that which is still beyond the limit of spiritual activity, the sensation or impression, and the actual æsthetic elaboration, which begins only when the mind becomes aware of the impression that has reached it through the channel of the senses.

We have mentioned, in connection with the identification of intuition and expression, the fact that every word that we utter is constantly preceded by an internal image; which is as much as saying that language is a perpetual spiritual creation, on the same plane as all our other expressions, and as art. We are accustomed to seeing dead words and syllables in grammars and dictionaries, and we consider them as something external, as a kind of instrument that we use and accommodate to this and that purpose. But words that grammarians study, through a naturalistic process, as independent elements of the linguistic organism, are really alive and full of their meaning only in the active context of speech. The reality of words is only in the individual spirit that speaks, and every word is new every time that it is employed because it expresses that particular, individual moment of spiritual activity, which cannot be the same as any other one. Philologists have been divided on the question of the origin of language for centuries, some finding it in the logical activity, others in a system of mechanical symbols and conventions, a few admitting the conception of language as a pure æsthetic creation only for a mythic, primitive period, which is succeeded in the history of every language by a period of development by convention and association. But, as in all other branches of spiritual activity, it is here impossible to draw a distinction between the problem of the origins and the problem of the nature of language: linguistic expressions have fixed themselves in the course of centuries and stand before us as a body of language, as a reality independent of the individual activity that produces the particular expressions; this is what prevents us from recognizing in the actual linguistic facts the same creative energy that formed the first words uttered by man.

In this reduction of the philosophy of language to æsthetics, Croce again follows Vico, who professed to have found the true origins of languages in the principles of poetry, who first asserted the functional identity of language and poetry. This theory, however, seems to clash with the existence of what we might call the implicit conceptuality of language, of which we are constantly made aware by our grammatical categories. The fact is that the relation between language and concept is the same as between intuition and concept: that is, on one side, language is the material of our reflected thought, and it would be impossible for the reflection to begin without or before the language; but, on the other hand, the concepts appear in language not as forms but as matter. In other words, to speak it is not necessary to think logically, but it is impossible to think logically without speaking. The grammatical categories are not real elements of language, but products of abstraction, of a purely practical character, of the kind that we shall soon have to examine in the rhetoric of the arts.

What may help us, in thus conceiving of the active and intuitive character of language, is a comparison with other classes of expressive facts. When we speak of musical or pictorial language, we are aware that we are using mere metaphors for the purpose of collecting certain general characteristics which are common to some of these facts.   The various musical grammars, the rules of harmony or of orchestration, are nothing but summaries of abstractions: in the presence of a certain music, or of a certain picture, we cannot forget the principle that no expression can give birth to a new expression without first undergoing a new creative process.   And this is as true of the highest forms of artistic expression as of the words which we use in our daily life.

A number of objections to Croce's æsthetics have been prompted by his use of the word intuition. To the reader who has followed our argument, it is not necessary to explain that Croce's intuition has nothing in common either with the mystic intuition of the Neoplatonists or of the ultra-romantics, or with the intuition which Bergson sub-stitutes for the intellect as the proper organ of absolute knowledge.   It is not a mysterious instru-ment of the mind, by which man can either come in contact with supernatural realities, or, renouncing that which is distinctively human in him, enter into the actual movement and life of nature.   The fact that Croce has spent so much time and thought in trying to understand this first, naïve, elementary grade of the theoretical activity, does not justify his critics in putting him in the same class either with romantic metaphysicians or with romantic naturalists.   That such a confusion has ever been possible is only a further proof of the immaturity and superficiality of a large part of our most solemn contemporary thought. It shows how it has been given to grown-up and apparently educated men, to read a book without knowing what its subject was, and without even being able to shield themselves behind the saving grace of silence.

An objection of a quite different order was raised by Croce himself, who found its solution in the elaboration of his philosophy of the practical, or of will. It can be said of the theory of art as intuition, that it reduces art to a form of knowledge, to a theoretical function, while what we look for in works of art is life and movement, and the feeling and personality of the artist, that is, something that is not theoretical but practical. The answer might be that the feeling is content and the intuition form; but such a dualistic point of view would in reality destroy not only Croce's æsthetics, but the foundations of his whole philosophy of mind. And we would be back at a position which we thought we had already criticised and surpassed. The truth is that intuition, and the personality, or lyrical character, of a work of art, are only different aspects of the same spiritual process, that where one is, the other too will have to be found. What we can abstract as the psychic content of intuition, since we have already excluded abstractions and concepts, is only what we call appetition, tendency, feeling, will—the various facts which constitute the practical form of the human spirit. Pure intuition cannot represent anything but the will in its manifestations, that is, nothing but states of mind. And the states of mind are that passion, feeling, and personality which we find in art, and which determine its lyrical character.

In order properly to understand this new point of view, it must be borne in mind that the lyrical character of the poetry does not however coincide with the practical passion of the poet: the relation between the emotion and the intuition is not a deterministic one, as of cause and effect, but a creative one, as of matter and form. The poetical vibration is different in kind from the practical one. If I grasp Croce's meaning correctly, the feeling and movement which we find in art is something that belongs intrinsically to the intuitive activity— it is the dynamic of the creative process itself. And in fact, what we look for in the works of art is not the empirical personality of the artist, but the tonality of his individual æsthetic activity, which is always new and always unmistakably his own,—not the rhythm of his passion but that of his vision or contemplation, of his intuition of the passion. Any other way of considering this relation would inevitably lead us back to the conventional distinction of form and content, to the attribution of æsthetic characters to the emotions themselves, and to a definition of intuition not as a simple and primitive fact, but as a combination of the practical and the theoretical, of will and knowledge.

I consider this deduction of the lyrical character of intuition as one of the points of Croce's æsthetics which opens the way to new problems and stand in need of further elaboration; but what is important in it, and already firmly established, is the recognition of this character, through which the whole doctrine of intuition gains a deeper and richer meaning, and becomes more apt to deal with the concrete facts of our æsthetic experience.

III. THE CONCEPT OF ART

Further determinations of the concept of art—Theoretical and practical
   activity—The progress of æsthetic theories—An American instance:
   morality and art—The typical—The ends of art—The process of
   æsthetic production—Relations of the æsthetic with the practical
   activity—The delusion of objective beauty—Aesthetic hedonism—
   The æsthetic value.

THE determination of the concept of art as pure
intuition would be little more than a verbal variation of older doctrines, if its validity and importance
could not be proved in the actual practice of thought
on æsthetic problems, in the study of the relations of
the æsthetic fact with the other facts of human
activity, and in the criticism of errors which have
invaded the field of æsthetic thought through a confusion of the æsthetic with the intellectual or the
practical. We shall therefore not be able to grasp
the new concept in the fulness of its meaning until
we have surveyed the whole ground of the philosophy
of mind: the æsthetic concept cannot be said to
be fully determined until we have a clear conception
of the other fundamental grades or forms of the spirit.
For the purposes of our exposition, we may however
anticipate a summary or scheme of the essential
relations, which will be more fully developed in the
following chapters.

116

We have already seen how the logical activity springs from the soil of the pure intuition; how the knowledge of the universal follows the knowledge of the individual. The æsthetic and the logic grade, of which the second implies the first, exhaust the whole of knowledge, the whole theoretical life of man. A third grade or form does not exist: not in history, which Croce still considered, in the first years of this period, as reducible to the concept of art, and differentiated from it only by its employment of the predicate of existence, of the distinction between reality and imagination; and not in the natural and mathematical sciences, which elaborate the data of intuition through fictions, hypotheses, and conventions, which are practical and not theoretical processes.

The relation between the theoretical and the practical activity is of the same kind as that between the two grades of the theoretical activity: that is, the first is the basis of the second. We can think of a knowing which is independent from the will, but not of a will which is independent of knowledge: it is impossible to will without historical intuitions and a knowledge of relations. Within the practical activity, we can further distinguish two grades corresponding to the two grades of the theoretical activity: the economic, which is the will of the individual, of a particular end, and the ethic, which is the will of the universal, of the rational end. The relation between the economic and the ethic activity is again the same grade-relation as between the æsthetic and the logic, the theoretical and the practical.

The concrete life of the human spirit consists in the perpetually recurring cycle of the four grades of its activity, which is the law of its unity and development. The concept rises from the intuition, and action from knowledge; ethical activity is not conceivable without a theoretical foundation, and the concreteness of a particular end. At the close of the cycle, the spiritual life itself becomes the object of a new intuition, from which a new concept and a new action are reproduced *ad infinitum*.

In the history of æsthetics, the errors deriving from the confusion of that which is distinctively æsthetic with other forms of theoretical or practical activity, present themselves as a series of doctrines, which can be considered as gradual approximations to the definition of art as intuition. It is not necessarily, or not only, a chronological series, but rather a succession of actual moments in the deduction of the concept of art. Empirical æsthetics recognises the existence of a class of æsthetic or artistic facts, without attempting to reduce them under a single concept; practical (hedonistic or moralistic) æsthetics makes a first attempt at interpreting them by putting them in relation with one of the categories of spiritual activity; intellectualistic æsthetics denies that they belong to the practical sphere, though failing to discover their precise theoretical character; agnostic æsthetics criticises all the preceding moments, and is satisfied with a purely negative definition; mystic æsthetics, conscious of the difference of æsthetic from logical facts, makes a new spiritual category of them, affirms their autonomy and independence, but mistakes the nature of their relation with conceptual knowledge. We are all more or less familiar with the various aspects of these doctrines, and it can be said that none of them (with the exception of the first, which is now represented by psychologic æsthetics) is now being held consistently by any responsible thinker. The truth of the intuitive theory, which we find adumbrated already in classical antiquity in the Aristotelian theory of *mimesis,* and of which artists and critics have always had a kind of obscure presentiment, is now implicitly recognised by all who have an intimate contact with and a sincere feeling for art and poetry. The literary and artistic development of the end of the eighteenth and of the nineteenth century has been accompanied by such a wealth of critical thought, that a conscious understanding of the nature of art is now much more frequent than in former ages. The forces that were at work liberating logical and moral thought from the shackles of the past, reacted vigorously on æsthetic thought, and helped to make it more and more independent from both intellectualistic and moralistic errors. It would be possible to extract aphorisms and meditations from the writings of the greatest poets, artists, and musicians

of the period, to show how common among them
was and is the knowledge of the spiritual autonomy
and of the intuitive character of art. But because
the task of the artist is not that of elaborating a
philosophy of art, and a good many critics and
æstheticians, on the other hand, have very little
experience of the actual æsthetic processes, we find
that though the other doctrines are discredited, yet a
number of prejudices which have their roots in
them are still current,—the artists themselves re-
jecting them, as it were, by instinct and not by
reasoning, and the critics and æstheticians clinging
to them because they help them to gain a fictitious
possession of that artistic reality which escapes
them in its purity and actuality. An intellectualistic
or moralistic critic can easily mask his lack of æsthetic taste, his fundamental ignorance of art, by
talking at length and with great solemnity about
unessentials. Artists and poets, on the other hand,
are apt to react to these prejudices by falling into
the errors of æstheticism, that is by attributing to
their empirical selves the freedom that belongs to
their function, and by denying in the name of art
the autonomy and dignity of intellectual and moral
values. In both cases, what is manifestly lacking
is a proper understanding of the meaning of logical,
or ideal distinctions, for which the artists, I suppose,
ought to be more readily forgiven than the critics,
though æstheticism may be as dangerous to art as
moralism or intellectualism are to thought.

A recent literary polemic in America offered some striking examples of these prejudices. A critic of the older school, in a discussion of the moral tendencies of the age, introduced a criticism of the proposition that art is not concerned either with truth or morality, by affirming that this negative proposition could legitimately be converted into the positive one: the object of art is to deny that which truth and morality affirm. The sophism of this conversion is based on a confusion between the two logical concepts of distinction and opposition. The critic was not deducing a logical consequence of the first proposition, any more than if he were interpreting my saying that I am not interested as a student of literature in the law of gravitation, as implying a disbelief in the law of gravitation: he was merely stating his own conception of art as a conceptual and moral function, and of the value of art as an intellectual and moral value; which is the error of intellectualism and moralism. In his reply to the older critic, a writer of the younger generation contended that æsthetic values are higher than either logical or moral values, and in some mysterious way transcend and comprehend them both. The younger writer was evidently using the same kind of logic as his adversary, and affirming on his own account the error of a variety of æstheticism.

What the original proposition actually implies is that judgments regarding the logical truth or the historical verity, the moral merit or demerit of a work of art, do not treat art as art, but dissolve the work itself into its abstract elements, and deal with these elements in an entirely different context.   If I discuss the theology and philosophy of Dante, I shall find a number of propositions which to my mind are untrue; but the beauty of Dante's poetry is incommensurable with the truth or falsehood of his logical thought.   The beauty of Francesca's episode is not impaired by the quite reasonable suspicion that the poetical idealization of a guilty passion might have a dangerous influence on weak and sentimental souls.

The imperfect distinction between art and logical or scientific truth is responsible for the critical prejudice of art as expressive of the typical.   The typical is a product of abstract thought, of the kind that is employed in the natural sciences. The expressions of art are essentially individual and particular, and when we consider them as typical, we merely use them as the starting point for our own abstractions, that is, for the purposes of a quite different mental process.   Similar to the concept of the typical are those of the allegory and symbol, which are mechanical constructions of the intellect, and which art is unable to represent unless it reduces them to the particular and concrete.

The confusion between art and morality, being ultimately founded on the supposition that art is not a theoretical function, but an act of the will,

gives rise to the theories of the ends of art, and of
the so-called choice of the subject. But the end
of art is art itself, expression or beauty, or whatever
other name we shall give to the æsthetic value,
just as the end of science is truth and the end of
morality is goodness; that is, the concept of end
coincides in every case with the concept of value.
And the artist cannot choose his subject, since there
is no abstract subject present to his mind, but only
the world of his own already formed intuitions and
expressions; which he can neither will nor not will.
This is the truth contained in the old idea of poetical
inspiration, which was merely another word for the
spontaneity and unreflectiveness of art. A choice
of the subject according to ends other than æsthetic
is a certain cause of failure. The only conceivable
meaning that advice as to the choice of a subject
may have, is a kind of artistic *know thyself*, a warning
to the artist to be true to himself, to follow his
inspiration, and that which is deepest and most
genuine in it. It is, however, a tautological meaning,
and the reverse of the one which is given to it by
the moralistic critic.

If it is impossible for us either to will or not will
our æsthetic vision, the internal image which is
the true " work of art," it is clear that an element
of will enters into the production of the physical
or external image, made of sounds or lines or colours
or shapes, which we call works of art in a naturalistic or empirical sense. The complete process of

æsthetic production is symbolized by Croce in
the four following stages: *a*, the impression; *b*, the
expression or æsthetic spiritual synthesis; *c*, the
feeling of pleasure or pain which accompanies the
æsthetic as well as any other form of spiritual activity; *d*, the translation of the æsthetic fact into
physical phenomena. The only true æsthetic
moment of the whole process is in *b*, which alone is
real expression, while *d* is expression in the naturalistic and abstract sense of the word. Such a conception clashes against a number of deep-rooted
fallacies, which in their turn are the source of innumerable æsthetic prejudices. It is clear, however,
that what we call a printed poem is no poem at all,
but only a collection of conventional black signs on a
white page, which suggest to me a number of movements of my vocal organs destined to the production of certain sounds; and again, that these sounds
are not the poem in itself, apart from my understanding of their meaning, from my re-creation of
the internal image which prompted their original
production now recorded in the pages of a book.
Physically, a painting is constituted by colours on
a wall, or board, or canvas: here, the first stage of
reproduction which is required for the written
poem is not necessary: the material (visual, as it
was auditive for the poem) on which the original
image fixed itself is directly present to me; and yet,
again, that material object is not the æsthetic
vision, but a mere stimulus for its reproduction.

Starting from the material object, Croce symbolized the inverse process of æsthetic reproduction in the following series: *e*, the physical stimulus; *d-b*, the perception of physical facts (sound, colours, etc.), which is at the same time the æsthetic synthesis previously produced; *c*, the æsthetic pleasure or pain. Here, again, the only moment of true æsthetic activity is in *b*, where, at least in the hypothesis of a perfect understanding, my vision coincides with the orignal creation.

It must be understood, however, that these successive stages are not real, but abstract or symbolical distinctions. We cannot re-create an æsthetic vision except through the sounds or colours in which it originally expressed itself; and those sounds or colours coincide with the original expression. The words and rhythm of a poem are to it what the body is to the soul, and once you have dissolved that form, there is nothing left. Hence the theoretical impossibility of a translation, which can only exist as a new creation. But when we consider those words or that rhythm not within the expressive synthesis, in which their reality is spiritual and not physical, but outside it, as words, as rhythm, we build up by abstraction a category of physical facts, to which we attribute a reality not inferior to that of the spiritual activity. *B* and *d*, in the preceding analysis, are not different realities, but different elaborations, the first, ideal, the second, naturalistic, of the same fact.

We have now established a relation between the
æsthetic and the practical activity: the physical
expression is an act of the will, and as such it falls
legitimately in the domain of both economic and
ethical judgments. We may buy or sell the physical
stimuli, books, statues, and paintings, though no
amount of wealth can give the æsthetic vision: the
possession of the objects of art is of another order
than the possession of the spiritual creation. We
may consider that the communication of a certain
intuition is in certain cases morally undesirable, and
censure the artist for having willed it, or try to
prevent him from accomplishing it. The principle
of the spiritual autonomy of art, necessary to establish the nature of æsthetic value, cannot be
understood to imply the absolute practical freedom of the artist from the laws that bind all other
men. But even from this point of view, there is
no doubt that art is more likely to suffer from excessive constraint than from excessive freedom; and
that the fanatics of morality in art are only too
often inclined to mistake a set of arbitrary rulings
for morality, and to overlook the intention of the
artist. It is a significant fact, and one which de-
serves more attention than it seems to have ever
received, that the so-called moral condemnation
of a true work of art has never outlasted one or
two generations, and their prejudices and weaknesses.

The existence of the physical stimuli or material

helps for the æsthetic reproduction, fosters the illusion of beauty as an intrinsic attribute of physical objects, first as artistic, and then as natural beauty. It is hardly necessary to criticise this illusion at this point of our discussion: beauty is not an objective attribute, but a spiritual value. In the same way as there is no intrinsic beauty, independent of our either creative or re-creative activity, in words or notes or lines or colours, there is also no category of natural beauty. What we call beauty of nature is either that which in nature is merely pleasureable from a practical and sensuous standpoint, or the presence of certain stimuli for the reproduction of a preëxistent æsthetic vision. We recognise the obvious truth of this fact, when we remark that the beauty of a certain landscape is not visible to everybody, but only to him who looks at it with an artist's eye. And it would be possible to write a history of the progressive development of beauty in nature, which would practically coincide with, or follow at a short distance of time, the various stages of the history of poetry and painting.

Closely related with the confusion between the physical attributes of the objects of art, and the true æsthetic value, are all the theories of æsthetics which consider that the end of art is pleasure, or æsthetic hedonism in its various forms. Of these the most ancient is the one that considers beautiful that which gives pleasure to the higher

senses, he hearing and the sight; and other forms
of it can still be found, if not among artists and
critics, at least among psychologists. Two of the
most recent interpretations of æsthetic facts, the
theory of empathy or *Einfuhlung* and the theory
of tactile values, are merely modern scientific variations of the old prejudice. But no hedonistic theory
can ever give a consistent account of æsthetic
facts, as it is impossible to draw a distinction, on a
purely psychological plane, between those pleasures
of the senses which may precede or accompany the
æsthetic fact, and those that are purely sensuous;
and the inevitable result is a complete reduction of
the æsthetic to the sensual. In such theories,
the real æsthetic problem does not even reach the
stage of being formulated.

The truth that the hedonist obscurely foresees
is that every spiritual activity is constantly accompanied by the practical reflex of satisfaction
and dissatisfaction, pleasure and pain, value and
dis-value. Value is every activity that unfolds
itself freely, dis-value is the contrasted, hindered,
impeded unfolding of the same activity. If we
call beauty the æsthetic value, then beauty is but
the successful expression, or better, the expression,
since an unsuccessful expression is not an expression
at all. And it is not necessary to repeat that by
expression we distinctly mean not the physical
stimulus, but the spiritual synthesis.

With this definition of æsthetic value we reach

one of the most important points of Croce's thought: the solution of what he calls the dualism of values, or ideals, to the concrete realities. As the beautiful expression is simply expression, the true thought is simply thought, and so on, so the ugly expression or the false thought are non-expression and non-thought, the non-being which has no reality outside the moment of its opposition and criticism.

IV. TECHNIQUE AND CRITICISM

THE relation between the æsthetic activity and the practical moment of the production of the physical objects of art may be regarded under the aspect of the relation betweeen art and technique. The only legitimate meaning of the word technique is that of a body of naturalistic knowledge in the service of the practical activity of the artist. In this sense we can conceive of a great artist who is a poor technician, as in the case of a painter who should use colours subject to rapid change and deterioration, a musician who should be a bad singer or pianist, a poet who should not be able to recite his own poetry. But in the common language of critics, we mean by technique something quite different—in painting what we call drawing or composition, in music, harmony or orchestration, in poetry, metre and construction. Now it is quite clear that we cannot conceive of a great painter who could not draw, a great musician unable to harmonize or to orchestrate, a great poet whose lines are defective. What we here isolate as the technical handling of an artistic subject is but the process of æsthetic creation itself, the succession and progression of intuitions in the artist's mind; using the naturalistic or psychological method, we abstract certain moments of the creative process, and we attribute a reality to such abstractions. We talk of the technique of a poem or of a painting as being something that has been superadded to the original intuition; we see the poet or the artist engaged in learning the technique of his art; we see him correcting or modifying his original expression according to certain technical standards. But what we call the technique of a poem or of a painting is that particular poem or painting in its concreteness; and no poet or artist can learn a technique except by re-creating in his own spirit the work of the great masters, his technical education being but one with his æsthetic education; and finally, the process of correction or modification is merely a stage of the expressive process itself: no poet can correct a line in his poem, no painter change a line or a shade in his picture, if the internal image has not first spontaneously undergone such correetions and changes in his mind.

The consequences of the common conception of technique in criticism are more dangerous, because more subtle and affecting a more intimate knowledge of art, than those of any other æsthetic error. The talk of the connoisseur and of the average musical or dramatic critic is full of such fallacies as the technical errors of great painters, the harmonic or orchestral wonders of poor music, the faulty construction of a great play; fallacies which may sometimes have originated from some real character of the æsthetic fact, but which are mere contradictions in terms. And the literary critic will speak of the *fine frenzy* and the *quiet eye*, meaning by the one, the abstract inspiration, and by the other the abstract production, and so miss the true æsthetic moment which is neither the one nor the other, but the synthesis of the two. Or he will oppose romanticism to classicism, in a similar sense, without realizing that all art is at the same time romantic and classic, truly inspired, and because truly inspired, able to express itself.

Mere variations of the naturalistic or psychological conception of technique, as an actual moment of the æsthetic creation, are a series of theories which Croce has extensively criticised, and of which we can give but a cursory account.

The theories of the particular arts and of their limits originate from the manuals of practical precepts useful to architects, sculptors, painters or musicians, and are founded on the assumed possibility of finding a field of the æsthetic activity corresponding to the physical means employed by each category of artists. But we have already seen that in the æsthetic fact there is no distinction between means and end: we can speak of the various arts in a purely empirical sense, as an external classification of the objects of art, but not as classes of æsthetic activity.

A similar kind of classification is the one which gives rise to the literary genre, and to similar abstractions in the other arts: legitimate instruments of work as long as we do not forget that there does not exist anything like the idea of a tragedy or sonata apart from all concrete tragedies or sonatas, and as long as we do not condemn a new tragedy or a new sonata simply because it is not like the old ones, that is, as long as we do not transform an abstract type into a law. Every new æsthetic creation, far from being bound to obey external laws, establishes new laws, or rather is its own law. It must, and will, answer only for itself, and the only claim that we can put upon it is that of internal coherence. Both the theories of the arts and the theories of the genres, when we try to treat them as true and rigorous, and not as mere practical expedients, manifest the absurdity of their task through their incapacity to give precise and absolute definitions. Every work of art expresses a state of mind, and every state of mind is irreducibly individual and new: a complete classification would therefore be only that in which every class has under itself a single intuition.

Another form of the technical prejudice is the creation of rhetorical categories, which are also abstract classes of expressions tending to trans-

form themselves into precepts. The main prejudice of rhetoric, in literature as well as in all other
arts, is that of the distinction between the simple
and the ornate, which is founded on a conception
of beauty not as the value of the expression, but
as something that can be added, so to speak, mechanically, to the expression. Because of its preceptive
character, rhetoric has done more harm in the history
of poetry and art, than any of the other classifications of the same order; and though it is generally
discredited among artists and critics to-day, in its
pure original form, yet rhetorical prejudices, both in
the creation and judgment of art, are still endowed
with an obstinately vigorous life.

These naturalistic classifications in art have their
counterpart in the study of language, in the creation
of grammatical genres or categories or parts of speech,
and in the attempts to reduce the empirical grammars to preceptive or normative grammars: that is, a
practical or pedagogic expedient, to a rhetoric or
technique of language. But the individuality and
indivisibility of expression is in the nature of language as well as of art, and language obeys not the
abstract precepts of grammarians, but the law of the
æsthetic spirit which makes us find a new expression
for every new intuition. Even phonetic laws, the
modern scientific instruments of grammar, are mere
descriptive summaries of observed facts, of physical
moments abstracted from their spiritual reality, and
therefore abstract or naturalistic laws, and never ac-

tually represent the concrete, individually determined facts of language.

A coherent theory of æsthetic (literary and artistic) criticism can be deduced from the concept of art as intuition, and we have already anticipated its main theses in the discussion of the concept itself. We have seen that in the process of reproduction of an æsthetic process, the actual moment in which the original image, through the medium of what we have abstracted as the physical stimulus, reproduces itself in a mind other than that of the creator (or, in what we might consider as a particular case, in the mind of the creator himself at a time other than that of the original creation), is a moment of æsthetic activity identical with that of creation. Given an identity of circumstances, that which takes place within my mind is the same æsthetic process which took place originally in the mind of the artist. If we call genius the creative, and taste the reproductive activity, the corollary of these considerations is that of the identity of genius and taste: in the act of contemplating and judging a work of art, our spirit becomes one with the spirit of the artist. Though in practice this identity may never be attained (because of variations in the material conditions of the physical stimulus, or in the spiritual attitude of the contemplator), yet if we deny it, and establish a difference in kind between these two aspects of æsthetic activity, we find ourselves inevitably led to exclude the possibility not of the æsthetic judgment only, but of all forms of æsthetic communication. There is a sense in which we can speak of the relativity of taste, and which accounts for the actual variety of judgments, not in relation to art only, but to all forms of human activity: every judgment is relative to our knowledge, at a particular moment, of the actual conditions in which the work of art was originally produced. But this is the intrinsic relativity of all the particular determinations of reality, not a relativity peculiar to æsthetic values, which are as real, though of a different order, as those of logic or morality.

But the æsthetic judgment itself is not the mere intuitive reproduction of the work of art, made possible by what we call historical criticism in the narrow sense of the word, that is, by interpretation and comment. These are the antecedent of the æsthetic judgment, which consists in a logical proposition of the form: "A is art," or "A is not art," "A is art in a b c, A is not art in d e f"; or again: "There is a fact, A, which is a work of art," "There is a fact, A, which is falsely believed to be a work of art." The æsthetic judgment, like all other judgments, establishes a relation between a particular, concrete fact, and a universal category, which is that of art. And, like all other judgments, it is at the same time a judgment of value and an historical judgment, which is the obvious consequence of Croce's identification of value and fact. Æsthetic criticism therefore coincides with the history of the æsthetic activity, with the history of poetry or art.

A frequent reaction to Croce's æsthetics, and to
its implications in the theory of criticism, especially
among literary critics, is a sense of irritation caused
by the loss of the so-called standards of judgment.
It would be interesting to analyze these supposed
standards, which generally are not explicitly enunciated (probably because their clear enunciation
would manifest their true nature, and annul them as
standards of æsthetic judgment), but only more or
less obscurely referred to with a mixture of pride and
reverence. They would then show themselves to be
the critical duplicates of the various æsthetic errors
which we have already discussed.

If the standards of which the critics speak are, as
is often the case, moral or intellectual ideals, it is
clear that Croce's æsthetics does not question their
validity, but only their application. There is a large
number of literary critics, who are such only in name,
and whose real interests are intellectual or moral,
critics of thought and of the ethical life, and not
of art. They use works of art as documents
and undoubtedly works of art are, in the unity of
the human spirit, documents of intellectual and
moral life; but their error begins when they confuse
the issues, and censure or praise the art of the past,
or try to influence the art of the future, with criteria
which are no longer intellectual or moral, but, because they have been transposed outside their legitimate sphere, intellectualistic and moralistic.

All other so-called standards are derived from the

abstract ideas of literary genres and of rhetorical categories. It is easy to judge of a new tragedy if you know what a tragedy ought to be, if you have a catalogue of purely external characteristics which you may either find, or not find, in the new work that comes before you. This is, of course, the crudest form of rhetorical criticism; there is another which is not less frequent, but more subtle. The critic builds up an ideal of what art ought to be, not with abstract categories, and classifications transformed into arbitrary æsthetic precepts or standards, but through his predilection for one particular author, or for one particular epoch, the Middle Ages or the Renaissance, the Classics or the Romantics: every work of art which is different either in spirit or in form from those that have been chosen is condemned in proportion to its variation from the ideal. This form of criticism is often also vitiated by the intrusion of intellectualistic and moralistic errors, since an ideal which is a mere particular determination of the past assumed as a universal value is likely to be mere rhetoric of thought and morality as well as of art.

The only legitimate standard in æsthetic criticism is the æsthetic standard, that of beauty or expression, as against ugliness or non-expression. Our critical judgment is the reaction of our æsthetic personality in the presence of a work of art, as the moral judgment is the reaction of our moral personality in the presence of an action. Our knowledge of a work of art, of a concrete and individual intuition, as our knowledge of an action, approaches more or less to the ideal limit, according to the breadth of our experience and the depth of our understanding; but there exist no external criteria on which we can rest our judgment, no mechanical props which will support it. This theory of criticism, far from justifying a capricious and arbitrary subjectivism, requires from the critic a constant vigilance against that which is narrowly personal, capricious, and arbitrary in himself; a patient, unceasing effort in the labor of recapturing and recreating the material and spiritual circumstances from which the work of art originally sprang; and the quick sensitivity of the artist coupled with the wide understanding of the historian and the philosopher.

When æsthetic criticism is raised to this plane on which it coincides with the history of poetry, or of art, it transforms itself necessarily into a general criticism of life. What to the æsthetic consciousness appears as ugly or non-expressive, since in the world of history there are no negative facts, will not, when historically considered, appear as a negative value, but as a value of another order, as an intrusion of the logical or of the practical spirit in the work of the poet or of the artist. What in the *Divine Comedy* is not poetry is the outcome of philosophical or moral preoccupations which have not become art, have not fused themselves into a new, coherent intuition, and must be apprehended not as art, but as philosophy and morality. The allegory of the *Faerie Queene* is not art, but it is an expression of certain aspects of the Protestant spirit in the England of Elizabeth. In a poet like Byron, the presence of practical motives is felt all through his poetical production; and the critic cannot limit his work to extracting the gems, and to saying of all the rest: this is not poetry. He must tell us what it is, and only by telling what it is, he criticises it completely as poetry. It is impossible, in fact, to give to art its place, without assigning its place to all the other activities of life. The great æsthetic critic will also be a critic of philosophy, of morality, of politics; but, as Croce says of De Sanctis, the strength of his purely æsthetic consideration of art will also be the strength of his purely moral consideration of morality, of his purely logical consideration of philosophy, and so on. The forms or grades of the spirit, which the critic employs as categories for his judgment, are ideally distinct in the unity of the spirit, but cannot materially be separated from each other or from that unity without losing all their vitality. The distinction of æsthetic criticism from the other forms of criticism, of the history of poetry and the arts from the other kinds of history, is but an empirical one, pointing to the fact that the attention of the critic or historian is turned towards one aspect rather than another of the same indivisible reality.

V. THE PURE CONCEPT [1]

WE have summarily examined in the three preceding chapters the theory of æsthetic, or intuitive,
or individual, as distinct from logical, or conceptual,
or universal, knowledge. We must now leave the
æsthetic activity in the background as the mere antecedent of the logical one, and proceed to investigate
the latter.

In a sense it may be said that the key to every
system of philosophy is to be found in the either
implicit or explicit solution given to certain logical
problems and that only by understanding the logic
of a philosopher can we be sure to give its true
meaning and value to his thought. The reverse is,
as a general rule, also true: any solution of a particular problem, any particular elaboration of the concept, when fully understood, will lead us back to the
philosopher's logic, to his concept of the concept.

The main points of Croce's logic could easily be

[1] See *Logica*, part i, "Il concetto puro," etc., pp. 1-170.

141

deduced from his æsthetics; but an untrained mind might unwittingly transpose the whole æsthetic theory on a purely psychological plane, and involve it again in the errors and contradictions of which it aims at being a conclusive refutation. A study of Croce's logic will render such a shifting of the perspective impossible. It will show that a discussion of Croce's æsthetics has no meaning except on the logical plane on which Croce has put it, and that therefore any serious objection to it ought necessarily to imply either a revision of the logical premises, or a demonstration that the actual logical processes are not rigorously in accord with these premises. What is here said of Croce's æsthetics is valid also for Croce's economics or ethics, and the reason is obvious. Croce's *Logica* is not a manual of logic, in a scholastic and formalistic sense: it is the exposition of his conception of the logical activity, and therefore the philosophy of his philosophy.

This method of approach to the logical problems, although unusual in our times, and antagonistic to the general tendencies of our culture, is not only, as its opponents assume, that of Kant and Hegel, but that of the whole tradition of European philosophy, beginning with Socrates, Plato, and Aristotle. It was only in epochs of philosophical decadence that logic reduced itself to a mere formalism or instrumentalism, to a doctrine of the means of thought, as opposed to its proper function, which is that of inquiring into the nature of thought, and therefore, since there is no way by which we can reach reality except through thought, into the nature of reality itself. To Croce, as before him to Hegel, the philosophical tradition is not a capricious sequel of unrelated speculations, but a series of connected efforts through which the human mind becomes progressively conscious of its own functions and structure. Nothing is more alien from him than that type of philosophical criticism, which exhausts itself in an attempt at reducing under a common denominator apparently similar solutions of problems, which in fact are profoundly different in their historical determination: but this consciousness of the historical factor in philosophy, far from breeding in him a sense of scepticism and of the relativity of truth, impels him to consider every effective thought as a necessary moment of truth, and to represent therefore the succession of effective thoughts, critically separated from what in the various concrete philosophies is merely postulated or imagined, as a perpetual integration of truth. This attitude explains why the immediate foundations of Croce's logic should be Kant's *a priori* synthesis and Hegel's dialectic, that is, the highest stages of the development of European thought before the positivistic antimetaphysical reaction which swept away for a time, not the last traces of transcendental metaphysics only, but philosophy and logic itself; and why also, among all the recent critics of Kant and Hegel, Croce should be one of the keenest and sharpest. His sure grasp of fundamentals made it easy for him to demolish all that is artificial and unessential in their systems; as is particularly evident in the case of Hegel, who emerged from Croce's criticism as the discoverer of one great principle and at the same time the creator, through the misapplication of the same principle, of many a false science.

This return to the philosophical tradition, which between the end of the last and the beginning of this century, was not limited to Croce and to Italy only, was accompanied and indirectly favoured by the researches of pure scientists on the method of exact and natural sciences. The economic theory of the scientific concept, such as it appears especially in the works of Mach and Avenarius, and to an understanding of which Croce had been prepared by his own studies on Marxism, was probably the most efficient instrument in destroying from within the pseudo-scientific constructions of positivism. The scientists themselves, by defining the limits of scientific thought, proved the impossibility of building a philosophy which should be at the same time a synthesis of all particular sciences and a system of reality. The conclusions of this new scientific methodology are on the whole accepted by Croce, and the fact that they naturally fall into their proper place in his logic is the most valid justification of his method, to which the distinction between the concept of philosophy and the concepts of the sciences is essential.

We need not point to the object of logic, or concept, as we did in a former chapter to the object of æsthetics, or intuition. The writing of this book implies a belief in its existence, and we could take practically any page of it as an example of what we mean by concept, or logical knowledge. We shall not therefore pause to confute logical scepticism, except by repeating the old argument that it is impossible to deny the existence of the concept except through the formulation of a concept. Such affirmations as that there is no other knowledge than the æsthetic one, or the one which is given by the ineffable intuition of the mystic, or by practical fictions, are in their turn neither æsthetic knowledge nor mystical intuitions, nor practical fictions, but affirmations, however contradictory in themselves, of a universal value and of an absolute character, that is, concepts. Through them, it is possible immediately to distinguish the logical form of knowledge, as represented by such affirmations, from the aesthetic or representative one, from the sentimental or practical state of mind of the mystic, and from those concepts which are mere empirical fictions. It is evident, in this last instance, that the theory of the fiction cannot be a new fiction, but must belong to an activity of a different kind, the logical activity, whose value is truth.

Of those three forms of logical scepticism, æstheticism, mysticism, and empiricism, the third one leads us to the distinction between the logical concept and the scientific concepts, or fictions.   The logical or pure concept is beyond all individual representations, and must therefore not contain any particular representative element; but, on the other hand, being the universal as opposed to the individuality of representations, it must refer to all and each of them.   If we think, for instance, of the concepts of beauty, truth, quality, development, and such like, it will be impossible for us to represent or imagine a sufficiently large fragment of reality that will exhaust them, or such an infinitesimal one as will not admit them.   This is what is meant by saying that the concept is at the same time universal and concrete, or, in other words, that it is transcendent in respect to every single representation, and yet immanent in all of them.   A third characteristic of the pure concept, besides those of universality and concreteness, is that of expressivity: being a product of knowledge, it must be expressed and spoken, and cannot be a dumb act of the mind, such as practical acts are.

The conceptual fictions, or, as Croce called them on account of their non-theoretical character, the pseudo-concepts differ from the pure concept in being either concrete and representative but not universal, or universal without any possible reference to individual representations, that is, without concreteness. The first class is that of empirical concepts, which contain some objects or fragments of reality, but not the whole of reality: such as the concepts of house, cat, rose. The second is that of abstract concepts, which contain no object or fragment of reality: such as those of triangle in geometry or of free movement in physics. The first are real, but not rigorous, the second rigorous, but unreal. Neither the ones nor the others can be considered as mistaken concepts or errors, since after having criticised them from a logical point of view, we still continue to use them for what they are; nor as imperfect concepts, and preparatory to the perfect ones, since their formation presupposes the existence of the perfect and rigorous ones: it would be impossible to conceive the house, the rose, the triangle, before conceiving quantity, quality, existence, and other pure concepts. It is true that in the actual development of thought, conceptual fictions have again and again given birth to true concepts; but in that case they have lost their intrinsic nature, and have assumed the characters of the genuine logical activity. In order to understand the proper function or nature of the conceptual fictions, it is necessary to fix our attention on the moment of their formation, which is practical and not logical. Their justification lies in their practical end and in their usefulness: they are instruments by the help of which we can recall with a single word vast groups of representations, or which indicate in a single word what kind of operation is required in order to find certain representations. The act of forming intellectual fictions is neither an act of knowledge nor of not-knowledge; logically, it is neither rational nor irrational (true or untrue); its rationality is of another order, practical and not logical. The activity which produces pure concepts, and that which produces empirical or abstract concepts, have been called respectively Reason and Abstract Intellect, or Intuition and Intellect; to which terminology Croce objects that the word intellect is certainly inappropriate to a non-theoretical activity. Croce himself is in no need of a new name for it, since he considers it one with the general practical activity, will or action.

The definition that we have given of the pure concept seems to clash against an insuperable difficulty arising from the multiplicity of concepts. If the concept is an elaboration of reality as a universal, how can we admit the existence of more than one concept? Beauty and truth are both concrete universals, and yet they are not the same universal: they have the same logical form, but they denote different aspects of reality. If this variety of the concepts, that is, of the aspects of reality, were insuperable, we should fall from the irreducible multiplicity of representations into a not less irreducible multiplicity of concepts, which would in the end justify a new logical scepticism and take us back to a mystical solution of the problem of the unity of reality. The passage from the multiple universals to the true universal would be logically impossible, and to be performed only by the help of some sort of mystical intuition.

The solution of this difficulty has already been hinted at in the discussion of the relations between intuition and concept, and between knowledge and will. The theory of the successive grades of reality, in their progressive implication, is the true form of the concept. Croce affirms the unity of reality, as a consequence of the unity of the concept, of the form through which only reality is known. But if we suppress the distinction, the unity that we reach is an empty and ineffable one: a whole is a whole only inasmuch as it has parts, as it *is* parts; a unity can be thought only through its distinctions. Therefore the unity and the distinctions are both necessary to the concept: the distinctions are not something outside the concept, but the concept itself, which is a unity of distinctions. The mind or spirit is one, but it is impossible to think of it as a pure and simple unity, outside of the forms in which it realizes itself, and of these forms in their necessary relations. Which is but a more comprehensive way of saying what we have already said speaking of one of those forms in particular, the æsthetic one, that it is impossible to conceive any of them except by determining its relations with the others.

It is necessary, however, not to convert these distinctions of the concept into abstractions: by approximation, and for a practical purpose, we can speak of a given action as a theoretical or practical one, an economic or moral one. In fact, in every fragment of reality we find the universal, and therefore all the forms of the universal. But on the other hand it is impossible to think any concrete datum, and to recognize it as an affirmation of the spirit as a whole, unless we distinguish each of its aspects in the most rigorous fashion. We shall then have a criticism of art and poetry, from the æsthetic point of view; or of philosophy, from the logical one; and a moral judgment which takes into account only the individual moral initiative. The distinctions of the concept are then used as directing principles of thought, but not, in the way empirical concepts are used, as criteria for a classification of objects; nor, again, as characteristics of epochs of actual historical development, which in the end reduce themselves to types of material classification.

Croce's theory of the unity and distinctions of the concept coincides with the old division of concepts into universal, particular, and singular ones. The true logical definition is reached only by determining the singularity of a distinction in relation with the other distinctions (particularity), and with the whole (universality). For instance, the concept of beauty is intuition (singularity), knowledge (particularity), and finally spirit or mind (universality). The symbol corresponding to this peculiar relation is not that of a line or succession, but of a circle: there is not a first and a last term of the series, a beginning and an end, but a perpetual revolution, in which every distinction in turn may appear as the beginning and the end of the series. Art or philosophy, knowledge or action, may be postulated with equal reason as the end of the spirit: the true end, however, is not any of the particular forms, but only the spirit or mind or reality as a whole.

Readers who are familiar with Hegelian logic will at once perceive the difference between Croce's and Hegel's treatment of logical distinctions. There is no attempt on the part of Croce to apply to them the dialectic process, which pervades the whole of Hegel's philosophy, and which is retained by Croce only in its legitimate sphere which is not that of distinctions but of oppositions. The dialectic process, of which the remote ancestor is Plato, and the more immediate forbears those Renaissance philosophers, Cusanus and Bruno, who more or less obscurely affirmed the *principium coincidentiæ oppositorum*, only with Hegel reaches its rigorous logical expression. The most famous instance of its application is to be found in Hegel's formula of the opposition of being and non-being, and of their unity in the becoming: the pure being is identical with the pure non-being, or, to say the same thing in different words, we cannot think the one without the other, and we do actually think the one and the other when we think the actual reality, which is neither being nor non-being, but becoming. Being and non-being are a true couple of opposites, as ideal and real, positive and negative, value and non-value, activity and passivity, and so on. By the application of the dialectic process, all these couples are shown to be not couples of concepts, but single concepts, each couple containing the affirmation and the negation of a single concept. Croce's criticism of Hegel is founded on an interpretation of the dialectic process as logically valid for such couples only, and inapplicable to the distinctions of the concept, or to empirical and abstract concepts; and this criticism, while emphasizing the importance of Hegel's main contribution to philosophical thought, sweeps away at one stroke all that in his philosophy has generally been considered as most distinctly Hegelian both by his followers and by his adversaries.

Croce's interest in such couples of opposites as those that we have mentioned is very far from being as keen as Hegel's. Their dialectic solution into single concepts is implicit in every phase of Croce's philosophy. This can best be seen in the constant interchange of such words as spirit and reality; each of them, when taken by itself, a pure, formal spirit, and a pure, material reality, are meaningless, while, once they have been correlated, both indicate the same concept, the spirit perpetually realizing itself in the concreteness of life: a formula which contains the whole of Croce's immanentism. But within the distinctions of the concept, the dialectic process is constantly applied by Croce to such oppositions as those of good and evil, true and false, beautiful and ugly, which are nothing but the double aspect,

affirmative and negative, respectively, of the concepts of goodness, and truth, and beauty. We need
only recall what we have said of Croce's conception
of æsthetic value, and of value in general. The
dialectic process is the logical structure of Croce's
concept of value. The positive element of each concept is the only real one, and a negative judgment of
value is not a purely logical judgment, but a statement to which is added the expression of a desire
or of an exigency. If we say: A is immoral, we mean:
A follows his own immediate pleasure (a logical statement), and also: A ought to follow a higher end (the
expression of a desire). A positive judgment of
value, on the other hand, coincides entirely with a
logical judgment, or a statement of fact. The opposition of value to fact is of the same kind as that of
spirit to reality; verbal and apparent and not logical
and real. The underlying reality of the opposition
can be grasped only through the distinction; what in
the opposition is a negative and therefore a mere
abstraction can never be anything but a positive
value of another order, a distinct form of activity.
The action that we have judged as morally evil, if it
is an action at all, belongs to the economic order, is
economically rational, directed towards a particular
end which confers on it its particular value; and the
same applies to all the other categories of reality, in
which error and evil cannot be introduced except by
the substitution of one form for the other. It is impossible to distinguish a concept from its opposite as

two concepts; but when a distinction is introduced, the opposition loses its negative character, and identifies itself with a distinct but positive value. Error and evil as such are never present except in the act that transcends them, in the conscience that, realizing itself in a higher sphere, turns against them and condemns them. It is superfluous to point to the importance that this process lends to the distinctions themselves, which are now seen at last not as mere logical instruments, but as the actual differentiations of reality, the necessary conditions of all life and progress.

The concept does not exist outside its verbal expression, but the relation between logical thought and language, because of the purely æsthetic or intuitive nature of language, is not of the rigorous character which is postulated by the Aristotelian logician, and, in more recent times, by the student of symbolic logic, who both assume language to be an essentially logical function. It would be impossible for Croce to fall into that extreme of idealism which is the common vice of the verbal realist, for whom propositions, judgments, or syllogisms have a kind of absolute reality of their own, independent of the mind that thinks them. It may seem paradoxical to assert that nowhere is Croce's realism more apparent than in his treatment of the verbal forms of the concept; and yet his criticism of the old logical principles and forms, running parallel to that of the rhetorical categories and genres in the field of æsthetics, allows him to reach the actual workings of the logical activity with much greater intimacy than is possible through any kind of formalistic logic.

The logical judgment, or concept, appears in two main forms: the definition, and the individual judgment. In the definition, the subject is one with the predicate, both being universal; in the individual judgment, the subject is an individual, the predicate a universal. "The intuition is the æsthetic form of the spirit," is a definition; "The *Divine Comedy* is poetry," is an individual judgment. The individual judgment is one with the perception, or perceptive judgment, with the historical judgment, and, for the reason given before, with the positive judgment of value; it is the last and most perfect form of knowledge. But the distinction between the definition and the individual judgment is not an ultimate and irreducible one. The concrete logical act is always an individual judgment, that is, the affirmation of the unity of the individual and the universal in relation to a particular subject; and every definition is an individual judgment inasmuch as it cannot be but the solution of a particular problem, individually and historically determined. The particular problem, the group of facts, from which a particular definition arises, is the individual subject of which the definition predicates the concept. This identification of the definition and the individual judgment disposes of the familiar distinctions of formal and material truths, of truths of reason and of fact, and of analyti-

cal and synthetical judgments; which all are reduced
to mere abstractions, partial aspects of the only logical act, consisting in the thinking of the pure concept,
as a concrete universal.

The practical imitations of the concept, or pseudo-
concepts, also may appear in the double form of
definitions and individual judgments. From the
empirical concepts we can form empirical judgments,
which consist in the inclusion of an individual subject within a class or type, and therefore can also be
called classificatory judgments. From the abstract
concepts, the passage to the individual subject cannot
be effected without the intervention of an empirical
concept, that is, without a previous reduction of the
individual subjects to classes and types: this reduction enables us to form empirico-abstract judgments,
or judgments of numeration and mensuration. The
function of these judgments is, as that of the concepts
with which they are related, not theoretical, but
practical: to classify or to enumerate is not the same
as to understand, though they are both essential
operations of the human mind. The corresponding
judgments are therefore called by Croce pseudo-
judgments, or practical imitations of the individual
judgment.

The reduction of the pure concept to the individual
judgment is the fundamental innovation of Croce's
logic. It entirely disposes of any form of transcendental thought, of an Absolute or a Universal as something beyond and above reality, and therefore of the

last remnants of metaphysics in philosophy. It means, translated into terms of common language, that there is no thought outside the thinking of individual minds, individually, that is, historically determined; and, conversely, that there is no reality outside the reality of thought, since the postulation of an external reality is nothing but one more act of thought. In the light of this doctrine, the relation between the intuition and the concept, between æsthetic and logical knowledge, can be restated by saying that while the intuition is the autonomous, creative mental act, by which the individual is known as individual, the concept is the autonomous, creative mental act, by which the individual is known as universal, that is, not simply known, but understood. Since Kant, an autonomous creative act of the human mind has received in modern philosophy the name of *a priori* synthesis, a synthesis which cannot be resolved into its components, or material elements, because its form, and therefore its true being, cannot be traced in them, but is imposed on them by the mind. Croce's intuition is an æsthetic *a priori* synthesis, through which the obscure psychic material rises to the light of consciousness; his concept, a logical *a priori* synthesis, in which the intuition is no longer form, but matter, subject to a new form which is judgment and reason. The *a priori* synthesis is thus employed by Croce as the peculiar dialectic process of the distinctions of the concept, the rigorous logical form of the double-grade relation between the individual and the universal, between intuition and concept, between knowledge and action, and, as we shall see in his philosophy of the practical, between the economic and the ethical will. It is, however, not a mere logical form, or rather, it is a logical form, because it is the actual process of the spirit, which cannot either know or act except by forming *a priori* syntheses (æsthetic or logical, economic or ethical), that is, by constantly re-creating itself and its own reality and values.

VI. THE FORMS OF KNOWLEDGE [1]

THE result of Croce's inquiry into the forms of
man's theoretical activity can be summed up by
saying that there are two pure theoretical forms, the
intuition and the concept, of which the second can be
subdivided for convenience' sake into the definition
and the individual judgment; and two modes of the
practical elaboration of knowledge, the empirical
concept and the abstract concept, from which are
derived the classificatory judgment and the judgment of numeration. Already in æsthetics we have
found no rigorous criterion of distinction between the
general intuitive activity of man, as it manifests
itself in language, and those empirically constituted
bodies of particular intuitions, which we call Poetry
and the Arts: every man is a poet and an artist,
though we reserve these names only for those among
ourselves in whom the æsthetic activity manifests

[1] See *Logica*, part ii, La filosofia, la storia, etc., pp. 171–269.

itself in a higher degree, dominates the whole life of the individual spirit. The concept and the pseudo-concepts are also elementary, fundamental forms of knowledge, of which all men partake: every man, as he is a poet, is also a philosopher and an historian, a scientist and a mathematician: but, again, we reserve these names only for the most conspicuous manifestations of those common spiritual activities, and form the empirical concepts of Philosophy and History, of Science and Mathematics. We may speak of vulgar knowledge and of pure or scientific knowledge, but only by approximation and without forgetting that the only claim to rationality and intelligibility on the part of pure knowledge lies in its relationship with the elementary forms, in the same way as Poetry owes its power and beauty to the language in which it spreads its roots. A particular treatment of these higher degrees of knowledge is not, therefore, logically justified; the problems that they present are the same that have been met with in the general discussion of the theoretical activity, and all they will have to offer will be but a confirmation, and in some points a clarification, of what has already been said.

As Art is intuition, so Philosophy is the pure concept: it is easy to see that all the formal definitions of Philosophy that have ever been given, as science of the first principles, of the ultimate causes, of the origins of things, of norms, of values, of categories, are mere verbal variants of the pure concept. Even the most materialistic and realistic philosophies, since matter itself or nature or reality are assumed by them as principles of universal validity, as concepts or ideas, fall within the limits of this definition. In this sense there is no philosophy which is not idealistic: the differences between one philosophy and another are nothing but differences in the elaboration of the pure concept. What follows from this identification of philosophy with the pure concept is that all philosophies are, of necessity, systematic, inasmuch as it is impossible to think the pure concept as a singular or particular one, outside its relations with the whole. This systematic character belongs to every philosophical proposition, and not only to the actual systems of philosophy: the solution of every particular philosophical problem implies a vision of that problem in its universality, that is, in the system. We are constantly reminded of this exigency by the fact that a new and original elaboration of particular problems does actually react on the whole of our thought; and that we are often compelled to revise our fundamental opinions by the discovery of a difficulty which at first presents itself in one sphere of thought only.

Of such a process, the whole of Croce's philosophy is a continuous exemplification, but nowhere so clearly apparent as in the progress of his conception of history. His first step had been that of reducing history to the general concept of art, thereby emphasizing the concreteness and individuality of history, as opposed to the abstractness of the natural sciences, the concepts of which, in that early stage, he could not yet distinguish from those of philosophy. In the *Estetica* the conception is still practically the same, history resulting from the intersection of art and philosophy through the application of the predicate of existence to the intuitive material. In his first *Lineamenti di Logica*, history appears as the ultimate product of the theoretical spirit, "the sea to which the river of art flowed, swollen by the waters of the river of philosophy." But in the same *Lineamenti* he had not yet arrived at the identification of the definition and the individual judgment, which in his second *Logica* constitutes the final form of the pure concept, Croce's original interpretation of Kant's *a priori* synthesis. Between the first and the second *Logica*, Croce wrote his *Filosofia della pratica*, in which he denied the duality of intention and action, as in the *Estetica* he had denied the duality of intuition and expression: an intention which was not also an action appeared to him, as we shall see, inconceivable. It was by analogy with his treatment of this duality, that he solved the duality between the concept (in the sense of definition) and the individual judgment, which was also a duality of philosophy as antecedent and history as consequent, as he perceived that a concept which is not at the same time a judgment of the particular is as unreal as an intention which is not at the same time an action.

These are the successive steps by which Croce

reached his doctrine of the identity of history and philosophy, one of the most discussed and of the least understood among his theories. We shall come back to it later. But a few more hints on its meaning can already be given here. It is clear that by introducing the predicate of existence as essential to history Croce had already abandoned the conception of history as pure, that is, non-logical, non-intellectualized intuition: but the predicate of existence is insufficient to form a judgment, without the addition of the other predicates, that is, of the whole concept. The predicate of existence can only tell us that something exists, but not what it is that exists: the determination of the singular, in its relations with the particular and the universal, is implicit in the historical judgment, even when it is not openly enunciated. Such judgments as: This thing is, or has been, seem to present the proper form of the historical judgment; no other predicates than that of existence are here visible, but my talking of *this thing* implies that I know what *this thing* is; the other predicates are concealed in the subject. Every historical statement is, therefore, a perfect individual judgment. Its concrete and individual character, which Croce had asserted in his early theory, is here maintained by the presence of the subject, though the subject itself, in history, is seen not in its intuitive purity, as in poetry, but as a concrete determination of the concept. The identification of philosophy and history is not so much the effect of a more intellectualized view of the historical processes, as of the progressive consciousness acquired by Croce of the inherent concreteness and individuality of the universal—of that realistic view of the concept as expressed by his elaboration of the logical *a priori* synthesis.

The old distinction between a subjective and an objective treatment of history receives a new light from the foregoing considerations. It is impossible to make history without judgment, and, therefore, history is in a sense irreducibly subjective. But the subjectivity of history is not the arbitrary and capricious subjectivity of the individual historian, who introduces his own passions and tendencies into the historical narrative: it is the subjectivity of thought, of the earnest and dispassionate research of truth, which coincides with the only conceivable objectivity. What we call objective truth is not reached by renouncing thought, but only by making our thought deeper and truer. The historian who permeates with his thought his recreation of the past (and if he did not, he would be recreating the past as poetry, and imagination, not as history) needs not add a judgment of value to his statements of fact: the identity of value and fact presents itself once more to us in the intrinsic structure of the historical judgment. Whatever the aspect of reality to which we turn our attention, true history and true criticism coincide.

A consequence of this identification of history and

philosophy is that the only legitimate divisions of history are those that correspond to the distinctions of the concept,—history of knowledge and of action, of art, of thought, of the practical activity of man; and that the relation among the different branches of history is similar to that of the distinctions of the concept within the concept itself: that is, the history of one particular form of human activity is nothing but the history of the whole spirit of man as it realizes itself under one of its aspects, a statement that we have already illustrated when speaking of the history of art and poetry. Other divisions of history are possible and useful, deduced from empirical concepts (such as the state, the church, the drama, the novel, society, religion, etc.), but they are divisions of practical convenience, mnemonic and didascalic expedients, and not rigorous distinctions. Empirical concepts are, in fact, in constant use in history, but as instruments, not as constituents of historical thought. History is of the individual *sub specie universalis*, and not of the practical generalizations. This peculiar function of the empirical concept in history marks the distinction between history and the natural sciences, the final irreducibility of history to sociology.

As history is reduced to philosophy through the identification of the historical with the individual judgment, so philosophy is reduced to history through the identification of the definition with the individual judgment. Since every philosophical proposition is an answer to a given question, and every question or problem is individually and historically determined, the whole course of the history of philosophy is in constant function of the general course of history. This is the truth contained in Hegel's formula of the identity of philosophy and history of philosophy, which had been revived in Italy, when Croce was meditating on these problems, by his friend Gentile: a formula which he finally accepted and transformed into that of the identity of history and philosophy, in accordance with his view of philosophy as a moment or grade of the spirit of man. The *a priori* synthesis which constitutes the reality both of the definition and of the individual judgment is, at the same time, the reality of both philosophy and history. The distinction between the two is a purely didactic one: in the first the emphasis is laid on the definition and the system, in the second on the individual judgment and the narrative. But because the narrative includes the concept, every narrative clarifies and solves philosophical problems, and, on the other hand, every system of concepts throws light on the facts which are present to the mind. The confirmation of the soundness of the system is in the power it displays to interpret and narrate history; the touchstone of philosophy is history. The concept, in affirming itself, conquers the whole of reality, which becomes one with it.

We shall deal more briefly with Croce's treatment

of the organization of the empirical and abstract
concepts in the natural and mathematical sciences
because his views coincide in their general lines
with the economic theory of science, which is the
view of scientific method elaborated by the scientists
themselves in the last decades, and differ from it
only in so far as they are comprehended in a vaster
system of thought. Croce's polemic against pseudo-
scientific philosophy, which was amply justified at
the beginning of his career, has now lost a good deal
of its actuality, since the ambitious attempts to
organize the concepts of science into a system of
ultimate truth have finally collapsed under the blows
inflicted on their authors by science itself, and are
now relegated into a few academic and journalistic
backwaters. On the other hand, there is no doubt
that his discussion of scientific methods, though
sufficient for his purposes, is far from being as exhaustive as his discussion of either art or philosophy.

The natural sciences are systems of empirical
concepts, that is, of practical elaborations of knowledge, and, therefore, they do not belong to the
sphere of theoretical, but to that of practical activity. This proposition must not be understood
as referring to the practical ends, or applications,
of science: action requires a knowledge of the individual fact with which we are to deal, and, therefore, the true antecedent of action is not science,
but an individual (or historical) judgment. The
natural sciences are not subservient to action, but

they are actions in the service of knowledge. Because of the empirical and pragmatic character of their concepts, it is impossible either to unify them in a single concept, or to divide them according to rigorous distinctions. The natural laws which they evolve are the same empirical concepts, which give rise to the creation of classes and types, expressed in a different form; their empirical character is confirmed by what Boutroux called their contingency, which is nothing but the reflex of their arbitrary formation. Even the most general of those laws, that of the constancy and uniformity of nature, assumed as the foundation of so much pseudo-scientific thought in the nineteenth century, is a mere postulate of practical opportunity, without which it would be hardly possible to construct any science: it is the first economic principle of scientific method, not an attribute of objective reality.

The truth of the natural sciences, that truth of which they and their empirical concepts are an abbreviated transcription, is the historical datum, the knowledge of actual individual happenings. History is the hot and fluid mass which the naturalist solidifies in the schematic moulds of classes and types. The naturalistic discoverer is, therefore, an historical discoverer and the revolutions of the natural sciences are steps in the progress of historical knowledge. The difference in method between history and the natural sciences is not due to the supposed difference between a higher and a lower reality (spirit and nature), or to the fact that nature has no history; nature is perpetual activity and change, that is, history, as much as the spirit, but the progress of nature is less clearly perceptible and less interesting to us than that of the human reality, and, therefore, an abbreviated transcription is more apt to satisfy our needs in relation to the knowledge of what we call nature than to that of the spirit. The nature that has no history, and which is opposed in dualistic systems of philosophy to the spirit of man, is not the actual, historical reality of nature, but the empirical concepts of the natural sciences, their classes, types and laws, conceived as an objective reality and substituted for that reality. In this sense, nature is not a special object, but only a method of treatment, as is proved by the fact that that same method, applied to the so-called higher and spiritual reality, by such sciences as psychology, sociology, or comparative philology, creates the same kind of naturalistic categories in the domain of the spirit. It is of nature in this sense that the idealist denies the real existence, since the time when Bishop Berkeley repudiated matter as a mere abstraction. And here again, the scientist comes to the support of the idealist with his keen awareness of the pragmatic character of his hypotheses on the ultimate physical constituents of reality.

It is through this theory of the natural sciences that Croce succeeded in eliminating naturalistic transcendence from his thought, and, singularly enough, his first impulse in this direction came to him from his æsthetic studies, through his criticism of literary genres, of grammars, of the particular arts and of rhetorical forms. He saw how through them "nature" introduces itself, as a construction of the human spirit, in the pure spiritual world of art; and having denied its reality in art, he proceeded to discover it everywhere not as reality, but as an product of abstracting processes. This must not be interpreted as meaning that the naturalistic method is an illegitimate hybrid: it has its uses in its proper place, and not less in the study of mind than in the study of nature. It is only by mistaking its constructions or fictions for realities, that we can be tempted to deduce from the natural sciences a philosophy of nature, or from the applications of the naturalistic method to art and to the history of man, an æsthetics or a philosophy of history. But the natural sciences themselves are not responsible for the errors of philosophical naturalism. That such errors should not be limited exclusively to philosophers, but very often appear within the body of sciences like biology or psychology or sociology, is easily explained by the fact that no scientist is a pure scientist: but poor philosophy does not become science simply because it finds place in scientific books. The quarrel between vitalists and mechanicists, for one instance, is a philosophical (or historical), not a scientific dispute: and it reveals itself, ultimately, as the opposition not of conceivable realities, but merely of different methods in the elaboration of the historical datum. The coherent and clear-minded biologist is to-day a mechanicist, not because mechanism is the essence of reality, but because it is the postulate of his research. The vitalist, on the other hand, is inevitably brought by the trend of his thought to abandon science and to become more or less deliberately a philosopher. It is enough to mention in this connection such names as Driesch or Bergson.

The fictitious or conventional character of mathematics is still more apparent than that of the natural sciences; and we shall not add anything to what we have said in the preceding chapter about the abstract concept, the non-concrete universal, which is the distinctive process of mathematical thought. The application of the mathematical processes, through the empirical concepts, to the historical datum, gives origin to what we have called the judgment of numeration (and mensuration), and to the mathematical sciences of nature. All that has been observed of the natural sciences in general is valid for these also. Their truth is still only the truth of the intuitive, historical datum of which the empirical concepts are practical elaborations; the addition of a further practical elaboration, the abstract concept, can add to their mnemonic or, as it is more often called, technical efficiency, but not to the value of their original content. This process, as the purely naturalistic one, can be applied to the human as well as to the natural reality, but it is evident that its usefulness decreases in the passage from the one to the other, following the same standards that apply to the natural sciences in general, those of the relative perceptibility and importance of the individual happening. It is at its highest in physics or astronomy, less notable in biology or economics; practically inexistent in psychology or sociology, the two sciences that suffer not less from the delusions of misapplied statistics than from the invasions of cheap philosophy.

Croce's theory of science, as we have already re-marked, differs from the generally accepted method-ology of modern science only in its context, which is usually agnostic in the pure scientist, while, in Croce, it consists in the affirmation of the pure concept, or of the autonomy of philosophy: a proposition with which the scientist *qua* scientist has no reason to quarrel. In both cases, the auton-omy of scientific thought is only relative, and the difference of context is a difference in the deter-mination of its limits. In both cases, scientific thought is recognised as thoroughly legitimate only within limits. The cry of the bankruptcy of science, of which we heard so much a few years ago, is as meaningless for Croce as for the pure scientist; science cannot become bankrupt except by over-stepping its logical limits, that is, by first ceasing to be science and becoming the ape of philosophy.

VII. THE THEORY OF ERROR [1]

ONE of the most original developments of Croce's
thought—a doctrine that does not owe its validity
only to its connection with the system, since we
can find it adumbrated already in such widely
divergent philosophies as those of Socrates and
Thomas Aquinas, of Descartes and Rosmini, but
which in Croce's system acquires a new and wider
meaning—is the theory of the practical origin of
theoretical error, which we shall briefly discuss in
this chapter.

From a strictly logical standpoint, every error
is mere privation or negativity, the opposite of the
logical value which is truth, and therefore inexistent
outside the moment of opposition. As there are
not two values in æsthetics, the beautiful and the
ugly, but one only, beauty or expression, of which
ugliness or non-expression is merely the negative
aspect, so in logic also there is but one value, thought
or truth, and error is non-thought, that which logi-

[1] See *Logica*, part iii, "Le forme degli errori," etc., pp. 271-421.

cally has no being or reality. There is no thought which is not a thinking of truth.

Let us pause for one instant to consider this last proposition, which at first sight undoubtedly has a somewhat paradoxical air. And yet it is impossible not to accept it, unless we are willing to fall into the most radical scepticism, which would imply a renunciation not only of every form of thought, but even, since there is no action which is not founded on knowledge, of every kind of action. If we believed that it were possible for our thought to think that which is not true, no external criterion or standard of truth could even be substituted for that which thought intrinsically would lack, since the apprehension of such external standards would in itself be an act of thought, and therefore suffer from the indetermination and uncertainty of thought itself. This belief in the validity of human thought is in fact, however disguised or even openly denied, present in every thinking and acting being: every thought, every action of man is an implicit declaration of this faith. And once we have consciously acquired it, as an inalienable, intrinsic characteristic of our whole spiritual activity, it is evident that it leaves no place for faith as such, for an obscure, independent faculty, a mystical intuition, different from and superior to our human thought, and which could mysteriously endow thought itself with the gratuitous gift of truth.

And yet, after we have denied the logical existence

of error, we are still confronted with the mass of positive errors which we can more or less easily identify in the course of history and in our daily experience. Positive errors, that is, affirmations of knowing that which we do not know, are real products of our activity: but since the theoretical value, truth, is absent from them, they cannot be products of the theoretical activity. They must therefore be products of the only other form of spiritual activity, the practical. Ignorance or obscurity or doubt are not errors; they are the inexhaustible matter to which the spirit of man is perpetually giving form and reality. To be aware of one's ignorance is in fact the first stage in the research of truth, the *initium sapientiæ*. Thought and truth are affirmation; the positive error is an affirmation also, which simulates truth. We cannot think an error, but we can pass from thought to action, by making a false affirmation, a purely practical affirmation, which consists in the act of producing sounds to which no thought corresponds, or, which amounts to the same, only a thought without value, without coherence, without truth. What we have qualified in its negative aspect as a theoretical error manifests itself in its positive aspect as an act of will, directed to a certain end, a practical act, and, as such, having its own rationality, which is neither logical, nor moral, but purely economic, consisting in the adequacy of that particular affirmation to the individual purpose by which it has been prompted.

Morality requires that the thinking spirit should realize itself as truth; and therefore the economic act which is error, though logically unreal, though economically useful, finds inevitably its ultimate sanction in a moral condemnation.

Though this doctrine may appear unfamiliar to the logician, yet we all constantly depend on it in our analysis of error. We know that error is due to the passions or interests of men, which cloud the intellect, and the more an error is foreign to our own ways of thinking, the easier it is for us to discover the practical motives which help us to explain it away. That category of errors which goes under the name of national prejudices, for instance, is transparent in its origins to every man belonging to a nation other than the one in which a particular set of such prejudices is commonly accepted. And other categories of errors, social, professional, religious, and so on, are of the same kind, affecting only certain classes of men, because of the passions or interests or traditions which belong to them by reason of their peculiar practical associations. In the field of politics, or in any kind of heated discussion, this research of the practical motive is even pushed to the extreme, and the bad faith of the adversary becomes an obvious axiom. In such cases, the same passions being active on both sides, the research of the practical motive is evidently not pure and disinterested, but is itself moved by a practical motive, and therefore likely to produce a new error, rather than a clear judgment. Therefore, though rigorously speaking there is no difference between the error which is a deliberate lie and that which is due to a more or less justifiable weakness, and there is no error which is not in bad faith, which is not due to a deliberate act of will, yet, from an empirical standpoint we may distinguish between errors in bad and in good faith, and recommend tolerance and indulgence for the latter kind. But tolerance is not indifference. Croce went so far, in drawing the consequences of his doctrine, as to justify the Holy Inquisition; and in fact all our modern advocates of religious and political tolerance have really shaken our faith in its methods, but not in its principle, which is that of the moral responsibility of error. The Holy Inquisition moreover was bound to clash with true freedom, which is not the freedom of error but the freedom of truth, because it placed its faith in a static, extra-human truth, as against the *veritas filia temporis*, the truth which is engendered and conditioned by history, by the peculiar problems and intellectual climate of the age, and which is the object of our modern faith; and therefore defeated its own end by striking at the roots of the value for the upholding of which it had been established.

Passing from the problem of the nature of error to that of the forms actually assumed by philosophic error, Croce accepts Vico's definition of error, as an improper combination of ideas, and therefore defines such forms, by deducing the number of possible improper combinations from his own conception of the legitimate forms of theoretical activity. This phenomenology of error is one of the main tasks of logic, while the refutation of particular philosophical errors is the task of philosophy as a whole. We shall rapidly survey these general forms, in which it will be easy for the reader to recognize the logical (or illogical) structure of many particular errors criticised in the preceding chapters.

The pure concept can be improperly combined with, or exchanged for, the pure intuition (art), or the empirical and abstract concept (the natural and mathematical sciences); or it can be improperly split in its unity of intuition and concept (*a priori* synthesis), and arbitrarily put together again, either as a concept which simulates an intuition or as an intuition which simulates a concept. Hence the five fundamental forms of error: æstheticism, empiricism, mathematicism, philosophism, and historicism or mythologism. To these must be added other forms originated from combinations of the preceding ones: dualism, scepticism, and mysticism.

We have dealt elsewhere with both æstheticism and empiricism. Of the first, the most recent form is that which pretends to build a philosophy of pure intuition or of pure experience, that is, of an experience which, not being touched by any intellectual category, is also pure intuition. Empiricism is practically all the current philosophy of our times, from the positivism of Comte and Spencer to the more modern types of the so-called philosophic elaboration of scientific knowledge. Mathematicism is a rarer and more aristocratic form of error: it does not consist in the application of the mathematical method to the exposition of philosophical concepts, which is a mere didactic expedient, more or less convenient, but insufficient to characterize the quality of the concepts themselves; its true exponents are those philosophers or mathematicians who take mathematical fictions, such as the dimensions of space, for realities, and proceed to speculate on such a foundation. The near future seems to promise a great extension of this kind of philosophy, through the prevailing interest in the theory of relativity, which is fondly supposed to contain the germs of a revolution in thought. Both empiricism and mathematicism lead to a dualistic conception of reality, by opposing either the facts of scientific and historical knowledge, that is, a collection of facts limited in space and time, to an infinite reality beyond that knowledge, or our actual world of space and time, to worlds, spaces and times mathematically conceivable, but of which we have no experience. The passage from this dualism to spiritualism and other kinds of superstition, which in our times seem to be so closely associated with certain forms of pseudo-scientific thought, is of the easiest. The naturalistic experiments by which we attempt to peer into the mystery of the so-called unknown or unknowable, hoping to detect the spirit itself as matter, however subtle or light, and such theories as that of the identity of the spiritual world with the four-dimensional space, are evidences of this immediate connection between superstition and science, for which, obviously, not science is responsible, and not ignorance even, but a chain of more or less deliberate errors in each case reducible to definite practical motives. From the point of view of the ethics of intellect, there is no difference between the frank impostor who is moved to speculate on other people's feelings only by greed, and the scientist who makes his science minister to his own private feelings, and is hardly, if at all, conscious of his fraud.

Of the other two forms of philosophic error, philosophism, consisting in the abuse of the purely logical element, and therefore in an usurpation on the part of philosophy against either history or science, tending to the formation of a philosophy of history and of a philosophy of nature, is less common now than in times of more active and original speculation. The most conspicuous examples are to be met with among Germany's classical thinkers; and we have already hinted at the connection between one particular logical error, the undue extension of the dialectic process to the distinctions of the concept, and to the empirical concept, which is the basis of Hegel's philosophies of history and nature. Both these sciences attempt an *a priori* deduction of the individual and of the empirical, a process which is in itself absurd and contradictory. They duplicate history and science with a series of concepts, which, unless they are the same which constitute history and science (in which case we have history and we have science, and not a philosophy of history or of nature), are necessarily empty of any concrete determinations. But though Croce points to philosophy of history and philosophy of nature as to the two typical instances of philosophism, yet he is ready to acknowledge that a good deal of thought that has gone under those names in the past has had a large influence in moulding many of our historical and philosophical conceptions, and, in the case of the second one, in helping us to realize the unity and spirituality of nature, and to recognize in the history of nature the same principles operating in the history of man. Croce's idealism, in fact, does not divide nature from the spirit except in the logical sense which has been made clear in the preceding chapter; it does not relegate nature in an unknowable sphere beyond the reach of human minds. It unifies spirit and nature, but *a parte subjecti*, and not *a parte objecti*, and reduces nature to the spirit, rather than the spirit to nature; which is the only process that makes such a unification intelligible and significant.

The last of the five fundamental forms of philosophic error consists in the arbitrary separation of the subject from its predicate, of history from philosophy, and in the consequent position of the subject as predicate, that is, of a mere representation as a concept. This may sound rather abstruse, but can immediately be made clear by adding that what Croce has in mind in this definition is the production of myths. This error he therefore calls either historicism (from the logical process by which it is produced), or mythologism (from the form which it commonly assumes). A myth is to him not a mere poetic or æsthetic imagination, but necessarily includes an affirmation or logical judgment. It differs also from allegory, in which the relation established between a poetic fiction and a concept is always more or less openly declared to be arbitrary, and the two terms are not confused with each other. In a myth, on the contrary, the poetic fiction assumes the actual function of the concept, transforming both philosophy and history into a fable or legend. Errors of this class are frequent in every system of philosophy, when the thinker, either consciously and deliberately, as in the case of Plato, or unwittingly, as in Kant's *Ding an sich* or in Schopenhauer's *Will*, fills the gaps of his real speculation with a mere image. But mythologism is more generally the form of religious error, since there is no religion without a logical affirmation embodied in a myth. If myth and religion coincide, as the distinction between myth and philosophy is that of error and truth, of a false and a true philosophy, we must conclude that religion as truth is one with philosophy, or, as Croce expresses it, that the true religion is philosophy; and this appears to Croce to be the conclusion of all ancient and modern thought in regard to the history of religions. Philosophies have sprung up in all times from the soil of religious thought, and more or less completely resolved in themselves, and logically clarified, the obscure substance of myth. This is Croce's clear-cut, unequivocal solution of the problem of the relations between philosophy and religion: there is no place reserved anywhere in his system for an either internal or external revelation other than that perpetual revelation of truth, which is at the same time history and philosophy.

From the possible combinations of these five fundamental forms of error, three more complex ones are derived: dualism, when two contradictory methods, one logically legitimate and the other illegitimate, or both equally false, are brought together, and considered to be both philosophically valid; scepticism, when the mind, in the presence of confusion and error, asserts the mystery of reality, which is the problem itself, but denies its own power to deal with it; and finally, mysticism, when even that last semblance of thought, by which the sceptic affirms that there is a mystery, is abandoned, and the immediate actuality of life is regarded to be the only truth. Dualism leads inevitably to the conception of a double reality, and we have already seen how the whole of Croce's speculation continually tends towards the logical unification of dualities, as with spirit and nature, value and fact. Every philosophical problem seems to present itself to his mind as involved in a dualistic difficulty; every solution becomes satisfactory to him only when the last shreds of dualism are eliminated from it. While scepticism is a logical error (the affirmation of a purely negative position), it contains within itself one of the essential moments of every progress in thought, the scepsis, or philosophical doubt, which is the negation of an error, and therefore the germ of every true affirmation. As for mysticism, we have dealt with it elsewhere as being one of the untenable aspects of logical scepticism; we may add that, if it ever obeyed the laws of internal coherence, we should not even be able to discuss it, since its only conceivable expression would be an ecstatic silence.

The same character of necessity that invests these forms of the logical error is present also in the false solutions of other philosophical problems, and we need only refer the reader to our discussion of æsthetic theories. In both cases, not only the number, but also the logical succession, of the necessary forms of error, depends on the number of possible arbitrary combinations of the spiritual forms, or concepts of reality. But infinite, on the other hand, are the individual forms of error, as infinite are the individual forms of truth: the problems are always historically conditioned and variable, and so are also the solutions and the false solutions, determined by feelings, passions, and interests.

From error to truth, there is no gradual ascent. The passage is described by Croce as a kind of spiritual conversion: the erring spirit, fleeing from the light, must convert itself in a researching spirit, eager for light; pride must yield to humility; the narrow love for one's abstract individuality, widen and lift itself to an austere love, to an utter devotion to that which is above the individual, becoming Bruno's *eroico furore*, Spinoza's *amor Dei intellectualis*. In this act of love and enthusiasm, the spirit becomes pure thought and attains the truth, or, rather, transforms itself into truth. And the possession of truth is at the same time possession of its contrary, of error transformed into truth; to possess a concept is to possess it in the fulness of its relations, and therefore to possess, in the same act, all the ways in which that concept, for instance, of the æsthetic activity, is at the same time the concept of hedonism, intellectualism, empiricism, and so on. The two kinds of knowledge, that of truth and of its contrary, are inseparable: the concept is at the same time affirmation and negation.

From this absolute possession of truth, we may distinguish a stage of research, which is not yet thought, but only the operation of the practical will creating certain conditions for thought. Seen in the light of this process, the series of errors through which a mind goes, when guided by a will to gather its materials and prepare itself to think, transforms itself into a series of attempts or hypotheses. An error is an error when there is a will to err; the hypothesis, however, into which the error is trans-

muted by the new will is not yet truth, and becomes truth only in the act of its verification; but
it is no longer an error, because it does not affirm
itself as truth, but only as a means or help for the
conquest of truth.

From this double consideration of the nature of
error, first, as error which is conquered and comprehended by truth, and then as attempt or hypotheses in the service of truth, Croce derives the identification of the history of error with the history of
truth, or philosophy.   But not in the sense in which
Hegel had considered the successive apparition of
the various philosophical categories and of the
various forms of error, seeing in them a kind of
gradual revelation of his own philosophy.   To
Croce such a conception of the progress of philosophy
is unacceptable.   Philosophy as an abstract category,
as one of the forms of the spiritual activity, has no
origin in time, is not limited to the men we call
philosophers, but acts in every moment of the life
of the spirit on the material offered by history, which
it contributes to create, and does not, therefore,
progress any more than the categories of art or of
morality.   But it progresses in its concreteness, as
art and the whole of life do; because life is development, and development is progress.   Every
affirmation of reality is conditioned by reality and
conditions a new reality, which in its turn is, in its
progress, the condition of a new thought and a new
philosophy.   In this perpetual cycle, though in-

dividual errors are conquered, no form of error can be definitely abolished; but they constantly reappear, because of the intrinsic necessity of their structure, and when they reappear not as wilful errors, but as attempts and hypotheses, they have their appointed function in the progress of truth and reality. To this constancy of error corresponds a constancy of truth: truth is not attained once and for ever, but is true in the act of its affirmation, and in proportion to its adequacy to the particular problem, to the individual conditions of fact, which necessarily include, at every given moment, the whole history of the past. Thus, from a different angle, Croce's theory of error reaches the same conclusion as his general theory of logic, the identity of philosophy and history; and philosophy appears as a perpetual development, a history that never can repeat itself, since every affirmation of the truth transforms itself into a new element of reality, into one of the conditions determining every new problem and every new solution.

VIII. THE PRACTICAL ACTIVITY [1]

Philosophical introspection—Affirmation of the practical activity—The
category of feeling—The theoretical activity as the antecedent of
the practical—Identity of intention and volition—Identity of volition and action—The practical judgment: philosophy and psychology—The problem of free will: liberty and necessity—Croce's
solution in the context of his philosophy—The practical value:
good and evil—The unreality of evil, and the function of ideals—
The sanction of evil—The volition and the passions—The empirical
individuality—Development and progress.

THE reality of the practical activity as distinct
from the theoretical activity, of will as distinct from
knowledge, can never be proved through the naturalistic method of psychology, by merely pointing
to a class of facts—actions—different from another
class of facts—thoughts. The so-called action
manifests itself, at a closer analysis, as infinitely
complex and rich in purely theoretical elements;
the so-called thought, as partly at least a work of
the human will. The concrete life of the spirit is
always both practical and theoretical, and the distinction we are looking for is an ideal distinction,
to be ascertained by the method of philosophical,
not psychological, introspection; by the direct
witness of consciousness, and by the deduction of

[1] See *Filosofia della Pratica*, part i, " L'attività pratica in generale,"
pp. 1–209.

its function in the concept of the spirit, or of reality, as a whole. The complete affirmation of a form, or grade, of spiritual activity is the philosophy of that form, and of its relations with the others; in this case, the philosophy of the practical, or of will. It is hardly necessary, at this stage of our exposition, to observe that the philosophy of the practical will not be practical philosophy, a collection of rules for the attainment of the useful and the good, any more than the philosophy of art is a collection of æsthetic precepts: it will be a purely formal science, a universal concept, the content of which is the infinite wealth of the individual determinations of the will, the history of the practical activity.

In the following chapter we shall deal more particularly with the two forms of the practical activity, economic and ethic, corresponding to the two forms of the theoretical, æsthetic and logic. Here we shall consider the undifferentiated practical activity, first, in its relations, and then, in its internal dialectic. The contents of this chapter are, therefore, intended as applying both to economics and ethics, to the useful and to the good.

There are two typical forms of scepticism regarding the practical activity. The first denies that it is a spiritual activity, by denying that man is conscious of his will, in the process of willing; consciousness comes only after, and is not consciousness of the will, but of our representation of the will. Therefore, the will is nature, and consciousness, or spiritual activity, is only our thought. The second does not exclude the will from consciousness, but affirms that there is no real distinction between will and thought. The first doctrine is evidently founded on a confusion between reflected and intrinsic consciousness; and maintains something that is always true of reflected consciousness, not in relation to the will only, but to every form of spiritual activity; carried to its extreme consequences, it would banish consciousness from the whole life of human mind, since every act of consciousness would always be consciousness of something else, and never of itself. Against this view, Croce insists on the concept of an intrinsic consciousness, which accompanies every act of the spirit: the consciousness of the creative artist, for instance, which is certainly other than that of the critic, but not less real. The will may be regarded as nature, only when apprehended by the theoretical activity; as every other act of the spirit becomes nature, outside its immediate actuality, when consciously reflected upon. The second form of scepticism, identifying thought and will, cannot maintain itself in its purity, because of the difficulties involved by the denial of what seems to be the immediate evidence of consciousness; it, therefore, qualifies itself by recognizing that the will is thought, but of a particular kind, thought impressing itself on nature, or realizing itself in action: which is but an indirect way of admitting the autonomy of the practical activity.

But do the theoretical and the practical activity exhaust the whole of the spirit of man? There is at least one more psychological category which clamours for admission within the precincts of philosophy, that of feeling or sentiment. For Croce, feeling as a form of spiritual activity does not exist: the corresponding psychological class covers a number of heterogeneous facts, which cannot be reduced to a single concept. Its function in philosophy has always been that of serving as a temporary term for that which philosophy had not yet fully determined and understood; in æsthetics, for the intuitive character of art, against the fallacies of hedonism and intellectualism; in the theory of history for the individual and concrete element of history, or even for the subjective historical judgment, against positivism and sociologism; in logic, for the pure concept against the empirical and abstract. Its function in the philosophy of the practical is of the same order: feeling or sentiment are among the names by which the peculiarity of the practical activity first began to be recognized, being labels for classes of psychological facts in which the moment of will is more important than that of reason, practice more essential than theory. But the psychological facts thus classified resolve themselves ultimately either into acts of knowledge or of will; and the witness of direct consciousness does not find feeling or sentiment within itself as a distinct form of spiritual activity. Obviously, this exclusion does not imply that Croce denies the existence of the empirical groups of facts gathered in those classes; it means only that he has reduced those facts to the immediate data of consciousness of which they consist, and divested them of that mysterious halo, the halo of ignorance or of deliberate error, with which an appeal to sentimental reasons is sure to be accompanied when introduced into a philosophical discussion. When we hear, for instance, that philosophy and science belong to the sphere of reason, and religion to that of sentiment, since there is no sentiment which is not either reason or will, we at once understand that what is meant is that the speaker is willing to believe, for practical motives, what his reason tells him to be untrue; and we know also that this error contains, sometimes at least, an element of truth, which is the affirmation of a truer reason than the one employed by a certain type of philosophy, by a rationalism which treats the human spirit as a thing of abstract logic. The error consists in the putting of one's will in the place of one's reason; the germinal truth, in the attempt to make one's reason wider, more comprehensive. It is, therefore, one of those positions in which it is a sin against the spirit to acquiesce, but which are the beginning of wisdom in the man of good faith.

The practical activity presupposes the theoretical activity: no will is conceivable without knowledge, and our will is such as our knowledge is. But this presupposition is of an ideal and not of a temporal order: the mind in its concreteness, at every moment of its life, is both practical and theoretical. The particular kind of knowledge which conditions our will is neither the purely intuitive nor the abstractly logical one, but the historical or perceptive, or concretely logical knowledge, which is at the same time a knowledge of things and of the relations of things, constantly changing with the perpetual development of the world around us, and, therefore, constantly re-creating and renovating itself as the antecedent of every particular volition. No other theoretical fact precedes the act of will: the so-called practical judgments or practical concepts, which some thinkers consider as a necessary intermediate step between the historical judgment and the volition, are nothing but classes of historical judgments relating to volitions in the past, mental formations similar to the rhetorical categories in the domain of art, and, therefore, do not really precede but follow the actual volitions. In the process of willing, the recognition of a certain action as good or useful, that is, as belonging to one of the practical categories, and, therefore, desirable, is not an act that precedes the volition, but is the volition itself. The qualification of an action as useful or good is not distinguishable from the volition except when it comes after the action, and is then a reflection on the act itself, not different in kind from any other historical judgment.

The conclusion to be drawn from these premises is that, in relation to every particular situation, intention and volition coincide; or, that what we call intention, the abstract volition, the imaginary volition, opposed to the concrete and real one, is not a moment of the will at all, and the only volition is the one that is determined by the concrete situation, the real and concrete volition. The distinction between intention and volition has in all times been the fertile ground for the growth of all kinds of hypocrisy, as it is easy to connect in one's mind a certain concrete volition, which is evil, with an imaginary intention of good; and the doctrine that justifies the means for the sake of the end is but a variety of this process. The identification of intention and volition is, therefore, not merely a matter of good logic; it is the necessary foundation of a realistic doctrine of the will, which cannot will anything but itself, and can never be abstracted from its real basis, from the actual determinations of the moment of reality by which it is conditioned.

Once the concrete character of volition has been recognized, there remains no difficulty in the way of further identifying volition and action. The relation between the two is analogous to the relation between intuition and expression in æsthetics: there is no volition which is not also an action, and vice versa. Volition and action are not two distinct phases of one process, but two different ways of looking at the same reality: the same fact which is, from the point of view of the spirit, a volition, is, naturalistically speaking, an action: we are in the presence of one more aspect of the old dualism of spirit and nature. And here again the duality vanishes when we observe that there is not a single act of will which does not manifest itself in a physical movement, however imperceptible, and that on the other hand there is no physical action, not even the so-called instinctive or habitual ones, which are not either direct or indirect products of the will. That which is independent of the will is not the action itself, but the success of the action,—what Croce calls a happening. The volition coincides with the action, which is the work of the individual, and not with the happening, which is collaboration or contrast of wills, the work not of the individual, but of the whole. No action ever realizes itself entirely in the happening, and no action, however hindered in its realization, is ever entirely without influence on the happening. The measure of the adequacy of the historical judgment preceding the action to the particular situation is given in some degree by the relation between the action and the happening; but it is impossible, and it is in fact never done, though we may affirm our inclination to do it, to derive the value of an action, of the actual, concrete volition, from its success. When we praise a practical hero for his success, we imply that his success was not accidental, not a mere happening, but entirely due to acts of his will; if the praise is misplaced, the error is not in the theory, on which we all implicitly agree, but in our knowledge and judgment of the facts of his life. And when we rise from the consideration of purely economical to that of ethical values, the importance of success gradually diminishes, because we fix our attention more to the spiritual reality, to the quality of the individual soul, and less to the material concomitants. The great majority of mankind's moral heroes would be utter failures from the standpoint of success, granted that it should be possible to speak of such a contradiction in terms as moral success, a phrase in which a true spiritual value, morality, is applied to a mere material abstraction.

The practical judgment, which is, as we have already seen, nothing but a particular kind of historical judgment, is a reflection on the action and not on the happening; and we shall not repeat here what has been said elsewhere of the relation between fact and value: the practical value is the action itself, and cannot be deduced or derived from standards, principles, ideals, which are but combinations of preëxistent judgments. The practical judgment, economic or moral, is a philosophical judgment in the sense in which every other judgment is also philosophical. A philosophy of the practical activity, not in the technical sense in which we speak of treatises and schools of philosophy, but in that universal sense in which every man is a philosopher.

as he is a poet, is therefore the necessary condition of the practical judgment. But this philosophy is fundamentally distinct from the psychological or naturalistic elaboration of the facts of the will, though at times it may have been materially connected with it. A psychologically descriptive science of the practical activity is, however, as legitimate in its own field as all other natural sciences; it constitutes a practical rhetoric which has as glorious a tradition as the rhetoric of literature, from Theophrastus to Spinoza and Descartes. It creates its classes or types of actions, the value of which is similar to that of all other empirical concepts, and by giving them a categorical form, it transforms them into maxims, rules, and precepts. As long as these types and precepts are taken for what they are, no harm can come from them; we all make similar formations as helps to our individual conduct, and find them more than helpful, necessary. But when they are taken as philosophy, then we have the usual results of this kind of logical confusion: either the empirical concepts, under a rigorous analysis, lose their consistency, and types or rules which were useful instruments for the treatment of particular problems are discarded for philosophical concepts, which are immaterial to the discussion, or they are treated as philosophical concepts, and invested with the character of universality and necessity which belongs to the latter. Of the first process, we shall give as an example the man who

maintains that war is necessary and eternal; which
is true, if by war we mean the perpetual conflict
and struggle which is the life of reality (a philosophical concept), but which is at least a gratuitous
assertion, when it is said of that particular kind of
war which is waged between state and state, with
arms and armies. Of the second, the moralist who
identifies morality with a particular system or set
of precepts, or the philosopher who turns his philosophy into a special pleading for his cause or party.

Turning now from the discussion of the relations
between the practical and the theoretical activity,
to consider the intrinsic problems of the will, and
the most complex and difficult of all, that of the
freedom of the will, we shall find that Croce's solution, though reached by a totally different method,
is very similar to the one offered by Bergson. Both
Croce and Bergson refuse to take sides in the quarrel
between free-will and determinism, but transfer
it to a higher or deeper ground where the contrasting terms acquire more significant, and no longer
opposite, meanings. Bergson accomplishes his abolition of the dilemma through a masterful psychological
analysis of the immediate data of consciousness,
Croce comes to the same result by applying to this
problem his logic of the distinctions of the concept,
which we have already seen so often at work. Every
act of the will is determined, in the sense that it is
conditioned by a given situation, and varies with
the varying of the situation; it is free, inasmuch as

it is something new and different, which was not given in the situation, and without which there would be no change, no growth, no development. Necessity and freedom, which so often appear as antagonistic views of the same fact, are both present, though distinct, in the volition, which is the unity of the two, being at once determined and free. The volition is thus regarded as a practical *a priori* synthesis, the autonomous creative act of the practical mind, as the intuition is the æsthetic, and the concept the logical *a priori* synthesis; the spirit never realizes itself except by acting, and it never acts except under given conditions of place and time. But as these conditions are nothing but what we have called happenings, which in their turn are complex results of single volitions, the concept of the freedom of the spirit coincides with that of its activity.

This solution is the one that we were obviously led to expect from the whole context of Croce's philosophy, a solution in keeping with his logic and with his general theory of knowledge. A similar parallelism we can observe in respect to the other solutions of the problem of the will: determinism is connected with a mechanistic materialism, as indeterminism with one form or other of mythicism. The doctrine of the double causality, which admits of a double series of facts, some subject to a mechanical necessity, others free and creative— a solution which is probably the most commonly accepted to-day—corresponds to the logical dualism of nature and spirit. This last one can be considered as an approximation to the abolition of the dilemma, as proposed by both Croce and Bergson, when we contrast it with the strictly deterministic position, though it still preserves the opposition of fact and value, of experience and philosophy, of reality and spirit. In the new conception of the will, necessity and freedom stand in the same relation as all these other dualities in Croce's system; and the emphasis is laid, as usual, on the second term, through which only we can understand the first. The agreement between Croce and Bergson in this particular instance points to a closer similarity between their respective philosophies than is apparent to a casual observer. That external reality which seems to confront the spirit as a separate existence, and which Bergson considers as the product of a purely mechanical, practical intellect, corresponds to what Croce defines as the naturalistic, not theoretical, but practical, elaboration of reality; and in Bergson's intuition and *élan vital*, Croce's concept of reality as spiritual activity is mythically adumbrated.

If activity is freedom, then freedom coincides with the value of activity. If we use the words good and evil, not with any special ethical connotation, but as the general terms of practical value and non-value, good and evil are activity and non-activity, freedom and absence of freedom. Evil, like all other purely negative values, is unreal. This does not mean that the actions that we call evil have no real existence, any more than the unreality of ugliness or falsehood imply the non-existence of bad poetry or of logical errors; bad poetry and logical errors have no æsthetic or logical reality, but they are products of the practical spirit, directed towards the satisfaction of practical ends; and every real action, inasmuch as it is an action, considered in itself as adequate to its particular end, is good. It is only by substituting to that end another end, that the first end may appear as evil, and the second as good; but if this substitution takes place before the action, then the action is inevitably directed towards the second end, and therefore again, it is not evil, but good. It is through a psychological delusion that we imagine ourselves in a position in which we see the good, and yet do the evil: what we do is that which appears to us as the most desirable end, and therefore as good. The intention, outside the actual volition, is, as we have seen, unreal; if it were real, it would realize itself as an action, and be one with it. The negative practical judgments, whether economic or ethic, are judgments which affirm the reality of a certain action, and therefore its value, at the same time comparing that value with a different one, which has not been realized in that particular instance. The negative moral judgment usually consists in the affirmation of a purely economic value contrasted with an ethical value which is absent from the action which is the subject of the judgment.

The doctrine of the unreality of evil has always been regarded with deep mistrust by the practical moralist; but that mistrust is utterly unjustified by the doctrine itself. For practical purposes it may be convenient to consider life as intrinsically evil, and to oppose to it a set of ideals, or abstract moral values to which we must strive to conform our actions; in fact, every one of us is constantly doing something of the kind, and finding in those ideals a help and an inspiration. But shall our ideals lose their value when we understand that they have no separate, transcendent reality? That every action carries its own value within itself, and that therefore unless we constantly realize those ideals in our concrete and individual actions, in every one of our actions, the ideals themselves will be but empty shadows? Every ideal, however high and comprehensive, is but an empirical concept derived from a class of actions in which we have recognised a moral value; moral standards have the same character as æsthetic standards, and are useful and active only as long as we understand their nature. But the creation of moral values is a constantly renovated, spontaneous, original activity, in the same sense in which art and poetry are. We can be directed, both in our activity and in our judgment, by standards and ideals; that is, standards and ideals may help us to put ourselves in a position practically favourable to the creation or judgment of æsthetic or moral values. But the actual creation, as the actual judgment, takes place, both in art and morality, so to speak, at the risk of our whole life: it is a new activity, in a situation which cannot be identical with any previous situation, and to which no rule will ever give us the key.

While on one hand our sense of responsibility is rather heightened than diminished by Croce's conception of value, if we look at the same doctrine from another angle, it tells us that there is no evil where there is no consciousness of evil; that evil becomes something positive, acquires an independent existence, only when it is reflected in a higher plane of consciousness. The only conceivable sanction of the evil that we have willed is in the will that, tending towards a better end, apprehends its former volition as inadequate and therefore evil; but until that light has shown itself to the spirit, all other sanctions are meaningless. This is the foundation of the Christian doctrine of repentance, of the uses of remorse, or grace; and the individual intimate quality of moral values was first proclaimed by the voice that said: *nolite iudicare.* If the Kingdom of Heaven is not within you, it is not to be found anywhere else.

We can consider the actual volition as intrinsically good, if we also approach it from the point of view of the multiplicity of possible volitions—impulses, passions, desires—striving to realize themselves at every moment of our life. Every single volition is the result of a struggle from which it emerges after having conquered all the other possible volitions. When, in this struggle, the single volition does not assert itself fully, we become the prey of that multiplicity, willing a volition which is not the one that we ought to will, and that in a way we feel we will; hence a will that is divided against itself, an action which is not positive but negative, not a true action, but a kind of passivity. When the single volition conquers the passions, when one impulse or desire becomes the will, all the other possible volitions lose their actual value, multiplicity gives way to unity, passivity to action, evil to good, death to life.

The passions can be empirically regarded as habits of the will, as inclinations towards one or another category of actions; by a further empirical elaboration, we can divide them into the various classes of virtues and vices, virtues being the passions or habits of rational actions, and vices the contrary ones. Individuality or personality, as an empirical concept, is nothing but a complex of more or less lasting habits, some natural and some acquired, or, more rigorously, the historical situation of the universal spirit in every instant of time, and therefore that complex of habits which historical conditions have produced. These habits are the material out of which we mould our life, and the first duty of every individual consists in exploring his own dispositions, in establishing what attitudes the progress of reality has deposited in him, at the moment of his birth and in the course of his individual life—to acquire a consciousness of what in religious terms we might call his vocation or mission; it is impossible for anyone to act except on the basis of his preëxisting personal habits of will. But temperament, or the empirical individuality, is not yet character, or virtue; and the respect that we owe to it, as the necessary condition of our action, must not be confused with the ultra-modern tendency which expresses itself in the cry for the rights of the individual temperament and for the free development of the passions. The individual has the duty of seeking his own self, but also that of cultivating himself in the light of reason; his empirical individuality is a mere datum, and his life is his own work. An education aiming only at the expression of individual idiosyncrasies (as so much of our modern education, at least in theory, is) is no education at all. The ideal is rather to be sought in such a perfect fulfilment of one's individual mission, however humble, that it should at the same time fulfil the universal mission of man.

The law of life is in the unity that conquers the multiplicity, in the will asserting itself above the passions. The reality is perpetual development, an infinite possibility transforming itself into an infinite actuality, gathering itself at every instant from the multiple into the one, only to disrupt itself again and produce a new unity. Multiplicity, contradiction, evil, non-being, on one side, and unity, coherence,

good, being, on the other, are unthinkable outside
the synthesis of life, which is activity, becoming,
evolution. This concept of becoming or evolution
is the one that modern thought has substituted for
that of an immobile reality and of a transcendent
divinity. And in Croce it becomes wide enough to
embrace Hegel's speculative dialectic on one side,
and the naturalistic evolutionism of the scientist on
the other. The dialectic of will is the dialectic of
reality, both spiritual and natural—or rather only
and always spiritual, since nature cannot be distinguished from the spirit as a concrete reality of
another order, but only as an abstraction of the praetical intellect. What we call life in nature is consciousness in the spirit, and the history of nature is
not qualitatively different from the history of man.
The whole course of history cannot be regarded
otherwise than as a continuous progress, a perpetual
triumph of life over death; and its rationality, which
we call Fate or Providence, is not the work of a
transcendent Intelligence, but is a Providence realizing itself in the individual, working not outside or
above, but within history itself. The mystery of
which we are all conscious is not a part of reality,
but only the presentment of future realizations, the
infinity of evolution. The God transcendent, the
empirical immortality, are mere figures and myths
for the God living in nature and in the spirit of man,
for the spirit of man, for the spiritual activity, which
is life and death in one.

IX. ECONOMICS AND ETHICS [1]

THE preceding chapter deals with the practical activity in general, with the general concept of will or action. We must now introduce in that concept a distinction analogous to that by which the theoretical activity has appeared to us first as the knowledge of the individual or intuition, then as the knowledge of the universal or concept. But here, again, we shall not employ the merely descriptive and psychological method, nor yet attempt to deduce this distinction from the analogy between the theoretical and the practical activity; we shall appeal once more to the immediate test of consciousness, which in fact reveals two distinct forms of the will, the economic and the ethic. Economic activity is the one that wills and realizes only that which relates to the conditions of fact in which the

[1] See *Filosofia della Pratica*, part ii, "L'attività pratica nelle sue forme speciali," pp. 211-319.

individual finds himself; ethical activity, the one
that wills and realizes that which, though related
to those conditions, at the same time in some way
transcends them. To one correspond individual, to
the other, universal ends; on one is based the judgment on the coherence of the action in itself, on its
adequacy to its individual end; on the other, the
judgment on its adequacy to universal ends, which
transcend the individual. If we recognise only
the ethical form, we perceive very soon that it
implies the other one, which we intended to exclude,
since our action, though universal in its meaning,
must always be something concrete and individually
determined. We do not realize morality in the
universal, but always a given moral volition, not
the abstract virtues, but the concrete works. Although a moral action is not only our individual
pleasure, yet it must be that, too, or we should
never be able to realize it. On the other hand, the
mere economic action, the satisfaction of our immediate pleasure, though it satisfies us in relation
to our individual end, yet it leaves constantly un-
satisfied that which we are beside and beyond our
individual determinations, our deepest and truest
being. And this dissatisfaction will last until we
succeed in lifting ourselves above the infinite succession of individual ends, and in inserting in them
a universal value. This passage or conversion from
the purely economic to the ethic, from pleasure
to duty, is designed by Croce as the conquest of

that peace which is not of a fabulous future, but of the present and real: in every instant is eternity, to him who knows how to reach it. Our actions will be always new, because always new problems are put before us by the course of reality; but in them, if we accomplish them with a pure heart, seeking in them what lifts them above themselves, we shall each time possess the Whole. Such is the character of the moral action, which satisfies us not as individuals but as men, and as individuals only because the individual is a man, and as men only through the medium of individual satisfaction.

The denial of the autonomy of the ethical form, the attempt to reduce the ethic to the economic, the morally good to the individually useful, is the substance of the many theories that go under the name of utilitarianism. But this reduction of the practical activity to a single principle clashes in every instant of our life against the distinction between mere pleasure and duty, between the useful and the honest action, between the things that have a price and those that have none, between actions which have a moral motive and those that have only a utilitarian one. The utilitarians themselves, unable to pass over the distinction, have tried to explain it away as a purely quantitative one, defining morality as the utility of the greater number or as the interest or egotism of the race; but it is clear that these so-called quantitative distinctions are really qualitative ones: the utility of the greater number is no longer individual utility or immediate pleasure, the egotism of the race is no longer egotism, but a value which transcends the individual. A further attempt in the same direction consists in considering morality as born from the association between certain acts which are means to a pleasure, and that pleasure itself: a savage fights to defend his personal liberty or his life, a civilized man, forgetting that the tribe, or the city, or the state, are but means to preserve his life and his property, defends them for themselves, and allows himself to be deprived of both his property and his life for love of his country. But only through stupidity is it possible to mistake the means for the end, and, therefore, this theory actually reduces morality to what is practically irrational, a product of confusion and illusion; that is, to the contrary of the practical activity, which is, in its own sphere, rationality and wisdom. The mere enunciation of this theory, if true, ought to produce the dissolution of those false associations, and, therefore, the destruction of morality; if morality subsists, this is due to its rational character, which associationism has not succeeded in disproving. The last refuge of utilitarianism is in theology and mystery: the utility of moral actions is not of this world, but derived from the conception of another world in which God punishes or rewards us for our conduct on earth. But this kind of utilitarianism puts itself outside the field of philosophy, by emptying the symbols of religion of their moral content, which is their only logical justification.

The converse form of error, which consists in eliminating the economic moment from the concept of practical activity, is criticised by Croce as abstract moralism. The economic moment has been regarded as purely technical, that is, as the theoretical moment that precedes action, action itself being always and only ethical; but some sort of knowledge precedes every action, and the distinction between the useful and the good cannot be reduced to that between knowledge and will; we can consider the useful as the means and the good as the end, only by forgetting that there is as much difference between knowing the useful and willing the useful, as between knowing the good and willing the good. The useful has also been identified with the egotistic and immoral; but the merely useful is amoral, and not immoral, in the same sense in which the pure intuition is alogical, and not either logical or illogical. The imagination of the poet cannot be submitted to the logical judgment, any more than the immediate pleasure of the child, or any action which precedes the awakening of the moral consciousness. And besides, the useful is so far from being immoral, that there is no moral action which is not also useful, as there is no logical truth which can express itself except through language. Finally, the useful has been defined as an inferior form of practical conscious-

ness; but what this definition actually accomplishes
is to recognise, though imperfectly, the true distinction, which is a relation of higher and lower only
in the metaphorical sense in which these adjectives
can be employed for the relation between the intuition and the concept.

Economics and ethics are the double grade of
the practical activity: it is possible to conceive of
actions having no moral value, and yet economically
effective, but not of moral actions which should not
at the same time be useful, or economic.   Morality
lives concretely in utility, as the universal in the
individual, the eternal in the contingent.   But we
can never sufficiently emphasize the true character
of the distinction, which, taken as a purely abstract
and psychological one, might justify the persistence
of morally indifferent actions within the moral consciousness.   The moral consciousness, once it is
awakened, invests the whole life of the practical
mind, as the logical consciousness does for the
theoretical mind, and it abolishes that condition of
innocence, in which the purely economic is not yet
subject to the moral judgment, in the same way as
perception and reflection destroy our naïve belief in
the reality of purely poetical imaginations.   On the
other hand, there are no actions which are economically indifferent, or, as they are generally called, disinterested; morality requires that the individual
should transform a universal interest into his individual one, make of morality itself his personal

utility, but it cannot ask for the abolition of all interests, which would mean the abolition of morality as well. The value of a moral action is in direct proportion with the passion and fervour with which we identify our individual ends with ends transcending our empirical individuality.

In the light of this distinction, the old oppositions of pleasure and duty, of happiness and virtue, lose a good deal of their rigour and sharpness. Pleasure as the positive economic activity or feeling can never be in real contrast with duty as the positive moral activity: a moral action brings with itself its own satisfaction or pleasure, and if it brings pain also, either the good action was not entirely good, not willed with all our heart, or it was accompanied by a new practical problem, which has yet to be solved. Similarly, happiness is not necessarily virtue, but there is no virtue which is not happiness; the sorrows of the virtuous are not intrinsic to morality, being but the limits of human activity, which the good share with the wicked. We all can transform our limits into sorrows, by our restlessness and unreasonableness; or, through resignation, our sorrows in limits and conditions of activity. Asceticism, which regards pleasure and happiness as essentially immoral, is the extreme form of moral abstractism; by destroying the economic category, it deprives morality of its reality and concreteness. It is, in fact, in the practical sphere, the counterpart of mysticism in the theoretical, which makes thought impossible by dissociating it from expression.

The recognition of the autonomy of the economic moment as one of the fundamental forms of spiritual activity, and the study of its relations with morality, appears to me as Croce's most important contribution to modern thought. We have seen what light the problems of the ethical will receive, when they are seen in their unity and distinction with the facts of the economic, or individual, will. We shall see in the next chapter what a vast field of human activity, comprising the whole political life of mankind, reveals a new rationality, once it is regarded as a legitimate product of the human mind, to be judged according to its own standards and values, and not to standards and values belonging to a different order of facts. Croce's discovery of the will of the individual as the first grade, the elementary form of the practical spirit, is analogous to Vico's discovery of the purely intuitive activity as the first grade of knowledge; and it establishes between economics and ethics, between politics and morality, the same relation as between æsthetic and logical values. The æsthetically true is the adequately expressive, as the economically good is the useful; but in both cases, we can never repeat it sufficiently, once the logical and the moral consciousness are awakened, neither the æsthetic can be apprehended otherwise than as logically true or untrue, nor the economic otherwise than as morally good or bad. The standards which are illegitimate when applied to art as art, to politics as politics, become rational again in the all pervading light of truth and morality. The predecessors of Croce in this line of his speculation are, on one side, the political writers who, from Aristotle to Machiavelli, attempted to define the relations between politics and morality; on the other side, the economists, who, by isolating a type of value, which was not an æsthetic, intellectual, or ethical value, and which could not be identified with the reverse of the ethical value, or egotism, had prepared the ground for the establishment of a philosophy of economics. As a matter of actual, historical derivation, it was from his study of Marxism, from his meditations on contemporary economic science, that Croce drew, as we saw in one of the first chapters of this book, his conception of economic value as one of the universal values.

After what has been said of the general relationship between philosophy and science, it will not be difficult to determine the place that *economic science* occupies in Croce's thought, in relation to his *philosophy of economics*. Economics as a philosophical science is that branch of philosophy, the object of which is the economic activity in its universality, the determination of the concept of volition or action as the volition or action of the individual, that is, as the predicate of the economic judgment or judgment of utility. The economic judgment, in its turn, is but a

form of historical judgment, and, therefore, the concrete form of the philosophy of economics is economic
history, the history of the spirit of man as it realizes
itself in the individual action or volition. Between
that philosophy and that history, there is no place,
as we know, for any intermediate form of knowledge,
but only for the practical (empirical or abstract)
elaboration, of the economic datum. This is what
the science of economics actually is: an applied
mathematical science, founded on empirical concepts. The postulates and types of economic science
are among the most perfect examples of conscious
fictions, beginning with the fundamental one of the
homo œconomicus: they are empirical concepts by
which the economic reality is simplified to such an
extent that it becomes possible to submit it to
mathematical calculation, and thereby to recognise
promptly its necessary aspects and consequences.
Economic science partakes, therefore, of the rigour
and absoluteness of mathematics, which is obtained,
as we know, only by sacrificing the concreteness of
its object. Its laws are arbitrary and tautological,
consisting, like all scientific laws, in the definition of
those characteristics of reality which have been abstracted to form its postulates or empirical concepts;
but it is only through the acceptance of such definitions that it succeeds in dominating, ordering, describing, and classifying the mass and variety of economic facts and, most important of all, in treating
them quantitively. It has, in fact, the same structure

as another science with which it has been frequently
compared, and which is here assumed as typical
of the proceedings of applied mathematics—mechanics. I believe that very few economists would
quarrel to-day with Croce's characterization of
economic science, since its mathematical character
is now universally recognised; but Croce proves
conclusively that even in its non-mathematical
phases, economics has always been a purely quantitative science. Volition and action are assumed in
it in their indistinction; and moral facts being volitions and actions as well as the economic facts,
they can also be included in the economic calculus,
because from a merely abstract point of view there
is no way of differentiating them from the latter.

Between the philosophy and the science of economics there is neither agreement nor disagreement,
but a total heterogeneity, and, therefore, a recip-
rocal tolerance. It is only when one invades the
field, or adopts the methods, of the other, that
conflict and error arise. Economics as a science
may then deny the legitimacy of the philosophical
study of the economic moment; or it may attribute
a universal value to its empirical concepts (as it has
happened again and again in the disputes between
free-traders and protectionists, or as it constantly
happens when economic laws are referred to as
endowed with a character of absolute necessity);
or, finally it may transform its fictions into realities, attributing for instance to the concrete human

being, and to the exclusion of any other quality, the qualities it has abstracted for the creation of its *homo œconomicus*.   But, in all such cases, though we may meet these errors among the economists, they are not scientific errors but logical errors; or rather, they are poor science only because they are bad philosophy.   The true function of the abstract economic schemes is that of an instrument in the hands of the historical and sociological observer, who needs many other similar instruments, if he wants to gain a concrete and direct knowledge of actual historical and social conditions.

It is now time for us to return, from this discussion of the two different elaborations of the economic datum, to a closer consideration of the second form of the practical activity, or of the ethical principle.   In the same way as the empirical concepts of economic science are insufficient to exhaust the infinite wealth of the economic principle, no single action or group of single actions can define the ethical principle, which is universal, and therefore merely formal.   By identifying the principle with a series, however vast, of particular determinations, that is, by substituting a material ethics for a formal one, we fall back inevitably into utilitarianism, since the volition of a single object or class of objects is not a volition of the universal but of the particular, not an ethical but an economic act.   Even the highest forms of moral ideals, such as benevolence, love, altruism, human-

itarianism, etc., once they are apprehended materially, and not as mere verbal approximations to
the formal ethical principle, acquire a contingent
and utilitarian character, and are apt to come in
actual conflict with the truly moral will. The same
criticism applies, and with greater force, to insti-
tutionalized ideals, such as the family, the state, the
social organism, the interest of the race, etc.; none
of them can be the object of the moral will without
exceptions and restrictions, that is, without losing
in the act of the will its institutional character,
and appearing as one of the particular conditions
under which the particular moral volition takes
place. The religious principles themselves are
subject to this reduction from the ethical to the
economic, when, as in the case of theological utilitarianism, they are taken as empirical limitations,
as particular objects, of the ethical will. The
material ethical principles are in fact analogous to
those material æsthetic principles which we have
criticised as rhetorical; they constitute a rhetoric
of the virtues not less deadly to the creative moral
will than the rhetoric of the arts is to the creative
intuition.

The ethical principle must be formal, but not
formalistic, and therefore Croce is not satisfied
with any of the so-called universal laws or categorical imperatives, or with any of the many formulas which attempt to define the moral actions
through one constant determination which ought

to be present in each of them. Such formulas
are mere symbols or metaphors, and can be used
as the equivalents of the ethical principle, as some
of the categories of material ethics can be used;
but their danger consists in giving the illusion of
possessing the true principle, while what we are
given is an empty and tautological one, which will
again give way to purely empirical determinations
and therefore to utilitarianism. This empty formalism, or absolute indetermination, of the ethical
principle, corresponds to two conceptions of philosophy, which Croce respectively calls partial and
discontinuous. According to the first, man may
know a portion of reality, but never reality as a
whole; as regards morality, he may hear the voice
of his own conscience, but never grasp with his
intellect the content of the moral law. According
to the second, he may know the reason of morality,
but not within the sphere of ethics, whose task consists only in establishing the moral law and deducing the moral precepts; the problem of the
essence of morality belongs to another science,
metaphysics. The reader who has followed us to
this point knows that Croce's philosophy is neither
partial nor discontinuous; that he does not admit of
any limits to human thought, nor of any division
in the body of philosophy. The whole of philosophy is already included for him in the first philosophical proposition, and though it may didactically
be useful to divide the problems of philosophy in

groups, or even to deal separately with the partie-
ular philosophical science on one hand, and with
general philosophy or metaphysics on the other,
yet truth does not belong to the distinctions outside
their unity, to the parts outside the whole, to the
segments outside the circle. It is this totality and
continuity of Croce's philosophy that makes Croce's
ethical principle a form, but not an empty one; a
form which is full in a philosophical and universal
sense, which is at the same time content, and universal as content not less than as form. He has
defined the ethical principle, not, tautologically,
as a universal form, but as the volition of the universal: a definition which is at the same time the
distinction of the ethical from the economical form,
or volition of the individual. We may here recall,
to test once more the coherence of Croce's thought,
and to make this definition clearer, his definition of
the concept as knowledge of the universal; by it
the concept is distinguished from the intuition, or
knowledge of the individual, and the logical principle
is seen as unidentifiable either with an abstract
logical form or with any particular system of philosophy. The concept is real only in the infinite
individual determinations of actual thought, as the
ethical principle in the infinite concrete volitions of
the human spirit *sub specie universalis.*

The universal which is the object of the ethical
volition is not something that we shall need to define at this point of our exposition, since the whole

of Croce's philosophy is nothing but a definition
of the universal.   The universal is mind or the
spirit; it is reality, as unity of will and thought;
it is life grasped in its depth as that same unity; it
is freedom, since a reality thus conceived is perpetual development, creation, progress.   Man, n
willing the universal, turns from his individuality
to that which transcends it, to the spirit, or reality,
or life, or freedom, not as abstract ideals, but as
they realize themselves in his individual action.
The volition of the individual, of one's individual
existence, is necessarily the first step; there is no
man, however deeply moral, who does not begin by
affirming his own individual life; without this
affirmation, he would never be able to transcend it
and to deny it.   But he who should limit himself
to this affirmation, and accept as a place of rest
what is only the beginning of his development,
would find himself in contradiction with his real,
intimate self. He must will not only his individual
self, but that self also, which being the same in all
selves is their common Father.   It is thus that he
promotes the realization of reality, lives the full
life, and makes his heart beat with the heart of
the universe: *Cor cordium.* *T*he moral individual
is conscious that he is working for the Whole.
Every action which is in accord with the ethical
duty is in accord with Life, and would be contrary
to duty and immoral, if instead of promoting life,
it should depress and mortify it. *T*he most humble

moral action resolves itself into this volition of the spirit in its universality. The soul of a simple and ignorant man wholly devoted to his modest duty is in perfect unison with that of the philosopher whose mind receives within itself the universal spirit. What one does, the other thinks; and both reach by different roads their full satisfaction in an act of life, in a fecund embrace with reality.

It is in pages like the ones from which we have extracted this enthusiastic definition of morality, that the true quality of Croce's philosophy is best perceived. But what is here affirmed as a principle lives as an ever present spirit in innumerable discussions of particular moral problems in his *Filosofia della Pratica,* in his moral essays, in his literary criticism (there is no living literary critic who has a keener perception of moral values than this implacable enemy of moralism), in the whole of his work. It is this moral enthusiasm, together with his capacity to see clear and deep, his catholic tolerance for all forms of beauty and truth and goodness, however distant from his tastes and inclinations, and his courageous, outspoken intolerance for all hypocrisies, compromises, half-truths, wilful errors, that has given Croce, in the last twenty years, in Italy, a right to moral as well as intellectual leadership. He is the true heir of an infinitely complex moral tradition, and placed high enough to do justice to all its elements, though apparently contrasting with each other. But when recognizing the symbolical and practical value of the various positive ethical systems that appear to him as gradual approximations to the full concreteness and universality of the ethical principle, he emphasizes the connection of his own ethics with one of those elements in preference to every other, with the religious and Christian element, for which morality is already what it is for the philosopher, the love and will of the universal spirit.   There is no truth of ethics which for him cannot be expressed in the words that we have learned as children from our traditional religion.   Between the religious man and the philosopher, between religion and philosophy, there is no enmity, but continuity and development; in the affirmation of the ethical principle, which is the crucial test of every philosophy as of every religion, the substantial identity of religion and philosophy is finally established.

X. THE LAWS [1]

ONE of the fundamental empirical concepts of the science of economics is that of economic society, which is formed by abstracting certain classes of economic relationships from the mass of relationships of all kinds among which the life of the individual realizes itself. Any treatise of economics can be considered as a definition of economic society; and we know how those definitions are apt to vary according to the choice of the groups of facts studied, and the method employed, by different schools of economists. The economic society of the Marxian is not the economic society of the classical economist; the Catholic economist, differing from both, will include in his treatment the consideration of certain ethical relations which give a greater complexity to his scheme. It would be possible to study the economics of the individual in perfect

[1] See *Filosofia della Pratica*, part iii, " Le Leggi," pp. 321–407.

isolation from all other human beings, limiting the elements of this particular form of society to one man, and that portion of nature from which he draws his food, his clothing, his shelter; on the other hand, the whole of mankind and the whole of nature may enter into a single, all-including, economic body. We may even study animal species, in their relations within themselves, or with man, or with other animal species, or with nature at large, from an economic standpoint (symbiosis and parasitism are facts bearing a close resemblance with human economy)—and thus form an infinite number of new economic societies. Each of these empirical concepts can be varied *ad infinitum*, by the mere inclusion or exclusion of certain classes of relationships.

The empirical, non-rigorous character of the concept of economic society is self-evident; and it can therefore be usefully employed to prove by analogy the similar character of the concept of society as manufactured by jurists, sociologists, and political scientists. It is against such fictions that philosophy reacts by building a concept of the isolated individual, that is, of the individual isolated from the particular classes of relationships which enter into the formation of particular empirical concepts of society; but it does this only to plunge the individual again in the midst of that infinite multiplicity, which is one aspect, and an essential one, of reality. Society as a philosophical concept cannot be identified with any form of economic or political society; of such, as mere abstractions, no philosophical treatment is possible. Society is that real multiplicity, without which we should have neither knowledge nor action, neither art nor thought, neither utility nor morality; and from society in this sense, the individual cannot be isolated, without reducing him, in his turn, to a merely abstract concept.

The sociologist, the jurist, the political scientist use their concepts of society for their purposes, which are, in the sense which is now familiar to our reader, scientific purposes. But very often they lose sight of the character of these concepts, and treat these instruments of classification and description as substitutes for the actual reality which they are, by reason of their abstractness, utterly unable to reproduce. The sociologist talks of the collective mind, and of collective representations, as if they had a reality outside the thought and action of the individual; the jurist builds a philosophy of law, in which society is opposed to the individual as a being to another being, and law, as a product of society, at every point transcends the individual will. The political scientist deals with the community, or the association, or the State, as with concepts of which it were possible to give a philosophical definition, valid for all times, and from which the rules of perfect government could be rigorously deduced. Of these types of philosophical degenerations of legitimate scientific thought, it can be roughly said that, because of the peculiar cultural development of the various nations of Europe, the first belongs more particularly to England and France, the second to Italy and Germany; though they are all more or less common in European culture as a whole. As an Italian, Croce was particularly interested in the second, the philosophical degeneration of juridical thought, and therefore his particular treatment of the economic facts underlying the problems of political society naturally took the shape of an inquiry into the nature of law. But it ought not to be difficult for the English or American reader, for whom these problems are not part of a practically inexistent philosophy of law, but of a long tradition of political science and theory of government, to translate Croce's thought into terms of his own cultural experience.

A law is an act of will, whose content is a series or class of actions. This definition excludes from the concept of law any empirical social determination; it includes within it all laws which are merely individual, the laws that the individual lays down to and for himself, the rules of conduct and programs of life and action, which the individual follows of his own accord. It may be objected that individual laws differ from social and political laws, because the latter are coercive and constrictive, while the former are not. There is no law, however, that is truly coercive; the individual is always free either to observe or not to observe the law. What a law does is to offer a choice or alternative, and this is as true of individual as of social laws. We may disregard our own rules of conduct or programs of action, and suffer from doing so, and inflict a punishment on ourselves for having done so; or we may alter our individual laws as social laws are altered when they no longer respond to the need of a community, and are either violently overthrown by rebellion or quietly allowed to fall into desuetude through non-observance, or modified by the proper organs of legislation. But the importance of the concept of individual laws lies in the fact that the so-called social laws have no reality outside the individual: in order to observe a law it is necessary to make it one's own, and to rebel against a law is to expel it from one's personality, of which it was, or tried to become, a part. The only real laws are, therefore, individual laws.

If the criterion of sanction or coercion is insufficient to draw a distinction between individual and social laws, we can still less use it to divide the social laws into customs or unwritten laws, and political and juridical laws. Both customs and laws carry with them sanctions, though of a different order, or, to put it in more precise terms, both offer a choice between probable consequences to the free individual will. This distinction, like every other subdivision of the laws (civil, penal, national, international, laws and by-laws, etc.), is a purely empirical one. But the concept of law comprehends these and many more in which the jurists have no interest, such as the literary or artistic laws (that a tragedy should have five acts, or, as at one time in England, that a novel should fill three volumes), or the rules of religious life, or the precepts of chivalry, down to the statutes of a criminal gang and to Balzac's *droit parisien*. In fact, the empirical distinctions of the laws are coextensive with the empirical concepts of society, and partake of the same characteristics: to the preceding examples of laws correspond respectively the republic of letters, a monastery, the order of knighthood, a band of robbers, and *le beau monde*. But the only reality, both of the society and of the law, is the individual assent.

The laws have one point in common with the so-called natural laws; both are concerned with empirical concepts, or classes. But while the natural laws are mere indicative statements of fact, the laws can always be translated from the indicative to the imperative; that is, they contain a volitive element which is absent from the natural laws. The volitive element is present, on the other hand, in the practical principles which have some time received the names of moral or economic laws, and which can be converted into such imperatives as Will the universal, or, in particular, Will the good, the useful, the true, the beautiful. But these principles are concerned with the universal, that is, with the spirit of man in the necessary forms of its activity, not with a particular product of the spirit, a class or type of actions, as do laws in the strict meaning of the word. This distinction between the practical principles and the laws opens the way to the recognition of a very important character of the laws: while the practical principles, because of their universality, have no limits and no exceptions (and we have already seen that a morally indifferent action is a contradiction in terms), the laws can never exhaust the universal, and therefore will always leave outside themselves a margin of actions, not included in any of the classes to which they refer, and therefore legally indifferent. In more technical language, we may express the same idea by saying that all laws, whether imperative or prohibitive or permissive (a law, according to the ancient formula, *aut iubet aut vetat aut permittit*), can be reduced to permissive laws: an order is always at the same time a prohibition, and both orders and prohibitions implicitly permit all actions which are not contemplated by the law.

Moreover, while the practical principles are immutable, always capable of giving form to the most varied historical material, the laws are in perpetual flux and change. The particular modes of change, whether by evolution or revolution, do not concern the philosopher, for whom all can be reduced to a single one: the free will producing a new law under new conditions. Against the perpetual mutability of the laws, due to the contingent and historical character of their content, clashes the concept of an Eternal Code, or Law of Nature (*jus naturale*), which presumes to determine the content and form of the laws, according to abstract reason, once and forever. This conception is due to an error with which we are now familiar, consisting in the transformation of empirical concepts into principals of universal validity. But from this particular error, as from all errors, we must distinguish certain elements of actual and concrete thought which have been historically associated with it. In the attempts to establish a Law of Nature, we shall then recognise either new concrete legislative programs, the new laws appearing as natural and rational by contrast with the old ones, or an attempt to deduce from, and through, juridical concepts, the principles of a philosophy of the practical. The principle of nationality, fighting for realization against the old dynastic law, appears to its defenders as a typical natural right; and Rousseau, when deducing the principles of the *jus naturale*, warns us that he is not dealing with historical truths, but with hypothetical and conventional reasonings, that is, with principles which transcend every particular determination and have not a positive, but an ideal value. We no longer speak of a Law of Nature, but the error which gave rise to that conception is still vigorous in current social and political discussions; every attempt to change legal conditions is always advocated or resisted by an appeal either to natural rights, which are but arbitrary rationalizations of historical con-

tingencies, or to abstract reasons, principles, or
ideas, of which the particular laws or institutions
are assumed to be the final and necessary expression.
But rationality, morality, and naturality, in the
sense in which these qualities are predicated of one or
another type of laws and institutions, do not belong
to any particular historical determination more than
to another; they belong only to the spirit of man and
to the concrete values that it realizes among the
everchanging conditions of history.

A law, being a volition of a class of actions, and
therefore of an abstraction, is in itself an abstract or
unreal volition. What we actually will is not the
law, but the single, individual action under the law:
the reality of the law is only in its execution. In the
individual execution, however, what realizes itself is
not the law, but the practical principle, economic or
ethic, of which both the observance and the non-
observance of the law are particular determinations;
the individual practical problems can never be fore-
seen by the law, which is by its nature general and
abstract. What is then, it may be asked, the use of
the laws? Croce's answer is that the laws are helps to
the real volition, in the same way as the empirical and
abstract concepts, though not real knowledge themselves, are helps to knowledge. In order to determine
ourselves to the single action, it is useful to begin by
fixing our attention to the class of which that single is
an element; in order to know either the individual, or
the universal, it is useful to create, between the

universal and the individual, classes and types, general concepts, or, as Croce calls them, relatively constant variables, through which the process of actual knowledge is made easier and quicker. We cannot think the pseudo-concepts, but they help us to think; we cannot will the laws, but they help us to will. The concept of law is akin to that of plan or design; in practice, a plan or design, and its execution, are one and the same thing, as we act by constantly changing our design, because reality, which is the foundation of our action, is in perpetual change. But this unreality of the plan, as distinct from the concrete individual action, does not deprive the plan itself of its practical uses, which are universally recognized, and which are identical with the uses of law.

When we identify the empirical laws with the universal practical principles, economic or ethic, we fall into "legalism," which can be defined as the belief that universal principles can be definitely embodied in a limited number of laws, and that, on the other hand, these laws partake of the character of absoluteness which belongs to those principles. It is especially in the treatment of ethics that this confusion has caused its worst effects. The two outstanding types of legalists are the Jesuit, who admits of the morally indifferent, the justification through the intention, the pious fraud, and other practical means for the purely literal observance of the law, supposed to be a sufficient satisfaction of the moral obligation, and the Puritan, who maintains that the unchangeable letter of the law is the only, and always certain, guide of the moral consciousness. Both Jesuit and Puritan, or to give them the names they assumed in a historical controversy, both Molinist and Jansenist, have often been in practice much better than their theories; but we are here interested only in their theoretical pronouncements, which, though apparently contrasting, yet combine in substituting the letter for the spirit, and in drying up, in the name of morality, the living springs of moral activity. And in both cases, moral legalism is associated with theological utilitarianism; it is, in fact, but another aspect of the same error.

The will that wills classes of actions, the legislative activity, is either moral or merely economic, and can therefore be judged as either moral or immoral, economic or anti-economic. But as the laws arc will in the abstract, our judgment of the laws will also be an abstract judgment. To pronounce a concrete judgment, we must turn to the moment of the execution of the law, to the individual practical action, in which the law realizes itself. In this sphere, it is vain to dispute whether a law is essentially economic or moral: the economic or moral character of the law is not determined by the abstract intention of the legislator, but by the manner of its execution, by the quality of the individual executor. The punishment which a law assigns for a category of crimes may be intended by the legislator either to deter or to emend the criminal; but in the man who abstains from that particular kind of crime, the law is an economic one if the abstention is entirely due to the fear of the punishment, it is a moral one if it coincides with a sincere abhorrence of the crime. No law, therefore, can be said to be intrinsically moral, and if we want to define the legislative activity in its full extension, we must define it as generically practical or merely economic.

The same definition obviously applies to the will that executes the law, as distinct from the will that formulates it: the juridical activity, as Croce names it, is also generically practical or merely economic, and as such united to and distinct from the moral activity. As the juridical activity, however, does not partake of the abstractness of the legislative, but is as concrete and determined as the economic activity, there is actually no possibility of distinguishing the one from the other; the juridical activity is therefore identical with the economic activity. This is Croce's original solution of the fundamental problem of the philosophy of law; a solution which is closely con-nected with his recognition of a utilitarian practical category, distinct from but not opposed to the moral category, and with his reduction of all laws to individ-ual laws. The reader must recall what has been said elsewhere of the relations between economic and moral values; and he will then understand in what sense it can be said that Croce's theory of law is an answer to the secular disputes on the relations between law and morality, between positive and ideal law, historical law and the Law of Nature. And he will also be able to perceive the difference between the reduction of the juridical to the mere economic activity, which, as we know, is also the form through which only morality realizes itself, and the theories of law as the pure embodiment of force and of the positive, established right as the only conceivable right, which are nothing but the counterpart of moral utilitarianism in the field of law. Croce's theory of law is, as all the rest of his philosophy is, a purely formal doctrine; not intended to defend one type of laws and institutions against any other, but attempting to furnish a conception of law, as an individual, perpetually new activity of the spirit of man, of which all laws and institutions, all phases and tendencies of political history, appear as concrete historical manifestations.

The philosophy of law has often had recourse to the philosophy of language for analogies by which its own problems could be clarified. A doctrinaire view of the juridical and political problem, for which the origin of law and society is to be found in an abstract convention, and which therefore tends to build up, by new conventions, a model legislation, or an Eternal Code, shows its real nature when related to the corresponding conception of language as a collection of signs, a purely symbolical organism, which can be so perfected by reason as to become an absolute, universal language, embodying in its signs every conceivable type of logical operations: a universal language, which should also be a universal symbolic logic. Sharply opposed to the doctrinaire, the traditionalist views certain types of positive laws and institutions as endowed with a character of necessity which puts them above the reach of the individual judgment of man; and as he fails to discover the ever present creative activity, by which man constructs his juridical and political world, he also withdraws from the human spirit the power to create its own language, and makes of words a divine institution. Equally remote from the sociological as from the theological concept, which are the extreme theoretical forms of popular errors, Croce establishes between law and language an analogy by which both manifest their intrinsic creative and human character. The reality of law is the individual juridical or economic activity, as the reality of language is the concrete intuitive activity. Law is the will of the individual, as language is the knowledge of the individual. Grammars and dictionaries are the codes of language, mere abstractions from the actual living flux of the creative expression, as the written laws and codes are but the grammars of law, mere abstractions from the actual living flux of political history. Language is not logic, and yet the logical thought cannot realize itself except through language; law is not morality, and yet the ethical activity cannot live except by incorporating itself in laws and institutions, and in the execution of laws, the concrete, individual life of institutions, that is, in the juridical and economic activity.

Thus, the end of this exposition of Croce's system, the doctrine of language with which the system opens links itself intimately with this doctrine of law, with which it closes. And both as regards language and as regards law, the last word is, of necessity, a new implicit affirmation of the identity of the philosophical with the historical method. The true history of a language is not a history of abstract grammatical schemes, but the history of the poetry and literature in which that language has realized itself, a history of individual expressions; the true history of law is one with the social and political history of a people, which is, and cannot be but the history of its practical activity in its effective, individual realization, that is, juridical and economic history.

PART THIRD
PHILOSOPHY AS HISTORY
(1911–1921)

I. WORKS AND DAYS

A retrospective view of the system—Germs of development—The return
to history—Croce's attitude during the war—Essays on the great
poets.

To the reader of the three volumes of the *Filosofia dello Spirito*, which were published before
1910, the whole of Croce's thought appeared as a
solidly constructed system, in which the four grades
or forms of spiritual activity were studied in their
intrinsic essence, and presented in their relations as
completing the cycle of living reality, in contrast
with that reality which the mind postulates outside
its living self, and which the system reduces to a
complex practical product of the mind, a collection
of material helps subservient to the essential forms
of its activity. Knowledge and action, reciprocally
implicated, are the substance of reality; and both
knowledge and action, rising, the first, from the
intuition to the concept, the second, from the economic to the ethical will, attain the universal, all-
including values which we express by the words
Beautiful, True, Useful and Good, but only and in
so far as they realize themselves in the concrete
and individual. A universal more universal than
that which is present in the individual act is inexistent, or exists only as an impotent abstraction

renouncing the concreteness and reality of the individual, and therefore also that true universality which has no being outside this action, this thought, this life. The soul of the system, slowly extricating itself from the traces of naturalism or intellectualism, which are still visible in the *Estetica*, is the logic of the pure concept, which resolves in the concrete universal the dualisms of nature and spirit, of fact and value, of life and thought, and, finally, of history and philosophy. But while this logic can be seen at work in all the parts of the system, and is, in fact, the form towards which all Croce's thoughts seem to have constantly tended from the time of his earliest philosophical essays, yet, to an attentive eye, it is possible to discover the successive stages by which it actually incorporated itself in the system. In particular, we have been able to point to the effects of the later meditations on the philosophy of will, on one side, on a more intimate understanding of the pure intuition as the lyrical intuition, on the other, on the identification of the definition with the individual judgment, and thereby on the relations between history and philosophy. On the whole it can be said that two apparently contrasting directions were at work within the system itself: one reflecting Croce's mental need for clear and fine distinctions, the other, that deep consciousness of the unity of the real, without which all distinctions tend to solidify themselves into dead abstractions.

If we imagine two students of Croce's philosophy,

endowed with antagonistic philosophical temperaments, the one a dialectician, the other a mystic, we
can easily conceive them as the founders of two
diametrically opposed schools of thought. The
first would have emphasized the rigorous distinctions,
the formal character, the intellectual precision of
the system; he might have retained the identification
of philosophy and history, but to him these words
would have stood only for the names of two formal
disciplines, and not for the concrete life of the human
spirit which is present in them. The second would
have passed lightly over the distinctions, and probably considered them as partaking of the same
unreality which belongs to scientific or legal abstractions; and by obliterating the logical processes
without which the mind of man is unable to grasp
and to express itself, he would have taken refuge
in an ineffable, though not necessarily silent, contemplation of the underlying unity. This hypothesis is not a criticism of Croce's philosophy; it is
merely the indication of the fact that, when the
system appeared as completed, new problems, and
therefore new errors or new truths, were bound to
grow out of the elements of the system itself. And
nobody was more conscious of this fact than Croce
himself, who concluded his volume on the *Filosofia
della Pratica* by expressly warning his readers of
the inexhaustibility of thought, which is one with
the infinity of reality and of life. No philosophical
system is final, because life itself has no end. Every

system of philosophy, being conditioned by life, can do no more than solve a group of problems historically given, and prepare the conditions for new problems and new systems. Of his own work in relation to his readers, he conceived as of nothing more than an instrument of work.

In these last few chapters we shall see Croce himself at work on the new problems generated by his own system, trying "more rigidly to eliminate the last remnants of naturalism, and to put a stronger accent on the spiritual unity," [1] yet constantly defending his conception of the spirit as the unity of distinctions, especially against the mystical tendencies of the new actual idealism. While never, in the course of his whole life, has he limited his activity to mere systematic thinking, during the last eleven years he has shown a more marked tendency to return from a philosophy, which is all a meditation of the formal problems of history, to those concrete works of history, by which he was started on his philosophical career; to return to them, however, with a mind in which the original uncertainty and obscurity has given place to a definite consciousness of the nature and purpose of history. The passage from the more philosophical to the more historical stage is marked by the publication of a fourth volume of the *Filosofia dello Spirito*, in which, under the title of *Teoria e Storia della Storiografia*, he collected a number of essays

[1] *Contributo*, p. 74.

written between 1912 and 1913, containing an elaboration of the theory of history already expounded in the *Logica*. This volume does not form a new part of the system, but rather the natural conclusion of the whole work, since the problem which it discusses is the one towards which tended all his former inquiries into the forms of the spirit, into their concrete life which is development and history, and the consciousness of which is historical thought. But before proceeding to analyze this final form of Croce's theory of history, we shall give a rapid account of the rest of his intellectual activity from 1910 onward.

As during the preceding eight years, the *Critica* continues to this day to be the main organ of Croce's work and influence, and in the *Critica* the greatest part of his writings are still published for the first time. The general features of the *Critica* have remained practically unchanged, except that his series of essays on the Italian literature of the last fifty years (which he collected in 1914–15 in the four volumes of *La Letteratura della Nuova Italia*) has been followed by studies on Italian historiography from the beginning of the nineteenth century to our day (since 1914), by essays on some of the greatest European poets (since 1917), by notes on modern Italian and foreign literature (since 1917), and by the *Frammenti di Etica* (since 1913), containing discussions of particular problems of contemporary morality. But practically all the reviews and essays published in the *Critica* and elsewhere are now being collected in the edition of his complete works, of which a full list will be found at the end of this volume. In 1912, for the inauguration of the Rice Institute in Houston, Texas, he wrote his *Breviario di Estetica*, which we have partly utilized in our exposition of his æsthetic doctrine, and which he reprinted in 1920 in his *Nuovi Saggi di Estetica*, which also contains his most significant philosophical essays of the last four or five years. His *Contributo alla critica di me stesso* ("Contribution to the Criticism of Myself") was written in April, 1915, on the eve of Italy's entrance into the war, and is the best essay in existence on the development of his thought.

Of Croce's attitude during the war we shall say but a few words. He was one of the very few European philosophers or scholars who did not transform themselves into improvised statesmen, or into passionate defenders of national prejudices and proclaimers of national hatreds. Differing from the Germanized philologist, who was the type prevailing in most universities before the war, in that he had not waited for the war to become aware of the many weaknesses and imperfections of modern German culture, while on the other hand he had lived for years in true and intimate contact with the great spirits of German Romanticism, he resisted with all his power the universal tendency of the time to make of the contingent issues of the war a criterion of intellectual truth and of scientific conduct. At the same time, his temper and education reacted violently against the false ideologies of the war, the superstructure of verbal ideals with which on all sides cunning statesmen and naïve philosophers attempted to veil the true nature of the conflict. Against these, he reasserted his conception of the political life and struggles of states as manifestations of the economic, amoral or premoral, activity, and of life itself as a perpetual struggle, finding its reason and its rest in the struggle itself. The theory of the state as justice appeared to him merely as a theoretical error, the fortune of which lay in the opportunity it afforded to give a convenient mask of morality to particular interests, either of individuals or of states. The intrinsic morality of the war he conceived as resting on its tragic reality, as reflected in a severely historical thought, to which it appears as a moment of that historical fate which crushes and destroys states as well as individuals, to create from their ruins always new forms of life.

It is needless to say that for a time at least Croce shared with Bertrand Russell and with Romain Rolland, two thinkers in many respects very distant from him, and yet as impervious as he was to the rhetoric of the war, the privilege of a vast unpopularity. Looking back now on his writings which were later collected in the volume *Pagine sulla guerra*, it is possible to discover among them many attitudes which were justified and useful only as a reaction against the current fallacies of the time; and also to realize that the man who speaks to us through them is not always and only a pure philosopher, but a man with a given complex of moral and political tastes and passions. But this is, in a way, as it should be; in the same way, between Croce the philosopher of æsthetics and Croce the critic of poetry, there is a difference which is inherent in the nature of the two different forms of intellectual activity; the philosopher is a man of understanding, the critic a man of tastes and passions. In both cases, his ideal has always been to make the critic or the moralist worthy of the philosopher, his particular comprehension of history adequate to his concept of the universal. To say that the equation is never perfect, is only another way of saying that every particular historical problem continually raises new problems of thought, and that Croce's thought finds therefore in itself the motives of its own development, the springs of its own life. Where passion and reason ultimately coincide, the roots of the development are taken away, and death takes the place of life.

Yet, notwithstanding these limitations, I know of no man whose thought on the war is on the whole more acceptable to those among us who lived through the war not as spectators, looking on it as on a vast moral abstraction, but as humble actors, in the midst of its human reality. A sense of collaboration between one side and the other, of being, here as there, employed in a common task, whose meaning was much deeper than any that had been offered to us by the national rhetoricians,—a collaboration which happened to take the aspect of a struggle, and imposed duties antagonistic, but of the same nature—was probably the most usual frame of mind among the soldiers who could think; and it existed, subconsciously, even among the unthinking ones, provided that their duties were of a definite, concrete kind, touched them in the deepest chords of their beings, involved the fundamental issues of life and death. To the man who consciously faces death, there is no comfort in wilful error; only this realization of an end that transcends all particular ideals, because it is the end of life itself, can be worthy of that price. You cannot willingly die for fourteen points any more than for one point, but death which is loathsome in the drama of mere circumstance, however adorned with brilliant rhetoric, is no longer death but an act of life in the tragedy in which the hero is conscious of his fate. There was no war, probably, that was ever more full than the last one of what might be called the material of tragedy; but what have the official celebrators done with it, they who have not feared to desecrate, in all our countries, one at least of the concrete, individual tragedies, in order to make of it an empty symbol, to transform an unknown hero into abstract heroism? In some of Croce's pages, there is a more concrete realization of the ideal

tragedy of the war than in any poem or oration that
I have seen to this day.

The last years of the war found Croce at work on
some of the greatest poetical spirits of modern
Europe, Ariosto, Goethe, Corneille, Shakespeare,
bringing to the understanding of their work, to this
task of concrete history, the deep consciousness of the
nature of poetry, and of the relations of poetry
with life, acquired in twenty years of philosophical
meditations. Even his functions as Minister of Public
Education during the last two years did not dis-
tract him entirely from his studies, and this year
of the sixth centenary of Dante's death was cele-
brated by him with the publication of *La Poesia di
Dante*, which will certainly remain as the most lasting monument raised to the memory of the poet on
this occasion. This troubled peace cannot make him
deviate from the path of his appointed labour any
more than the war could; in peace as in war, his duty
is his daily task, here and to-day, and his confidence
in the morality and usefulness of that work which is
his work is as little shaken by the prophets of despair
in peace, as it was by the messiahs of the promised
land who were so loud above the turmoil of war. He
is probably now noting with a smile that the same men
who talked of the war to end all wars, are now very
busy preventing our civilization from dying away;
that is, building a peace in the abstract, with programs and words, as they fought a war which was
not the war, but a phantasm of their imagination.

II. THE THEORY OF HISTORY

Two meanings of the word history—History as contemporary history—
    History and chronicle—The spirit as history—Philology, and philo-
    logical history—Poetical and rhetorical history—Universal history—
    The universality of history· history and philosophy—The unity of
    thought—Philosophy as methodology—The positivity of history—
    The humanity of history—Distinctions and divisions—The history
    of nature.

THERE are two meanings to the word history, in
English as well as in other European languages; on
one hand it denotes the actual doing, the immediacy of life, on the other, the thinking that seems to
follow the doing, the consciousness of life. In a
rough, approximate way, we speak of men who make
history, and of other men who think or write history—though we are all perfectly aware of the fact
that we cannot make history without first thinking
history, that the action, in other words, follows a
judgment of the situation, which is an elementary
form of historical thought, and is accompanied by
its own consciousness, which is its immediate history.
In this sense, the action cannot be materially severed
from its history: the distinction between the two is a
purely formal and ideal one. And again, the thinking of history, in the second meaning of the word,
consists in making present to our spirit, in re-living,

253

an action or group of actions, which thus become
as actual an experience as any practical doing, a
fragment of our own life, and, ultimately, the consciousness of our own individual experience.   Thus
the two meanings which stand out as sharply contrasting when we objectify and solidify them, as an
external, chronological series of happenings, and
as a formal discipline attempting to give, in innumerable books, a description and as it were a
verbal duplicate of that series, once we examine
them in the light of our consciousness, reveal themselves merely as different aspects or moments of
the same spiritual process.

Croce's latest writings on history may be puzzling
to the average reader because this ambiguity cannot
be overcome by him unless he is willing to penetrate
to the heart of Croce's doctrine, in which the word
history acquires a more pregnant and fundamental
meaning.   In many of us there is a tendency to balk
at any attempt at filling old words with deeper and
more precise connotations; but philosophy is not
a matter of words.   A new thought will in any case
alter the whole physiognomy of our vocabulary,
and to stand up for the old meanings is as much
as to refuse to think, or rather, to refuse to live.
For history as a formal discipline, for the actual
writing of history, Croce uses the word Historiography; but in his *Teoria e Storia della Storiografia*
(Theory and History of the writing of History), history still means both the doing and the thinking,

life and the consciousness of life, though not in the abstract distinction in which these meanings are generally apprehended. In Croce the distinction is also unity, and there is no doing which is not also a thinking, no life which is not also the consciousness of life, no consciousness which is not also the consciousness of itself. The ambiguity, some traces of which could still be seen in the *Logica*, entirely disappears in this fourth volume of the system, at least for the reader who has followed the whole development of Croce's thought.

We call contemporary history the history that is being made, rather loosely including in it a more or less extended stretch of time up to the actual present. But contemporary history rigorously ought to be only history in the actual making, the immediate present and the consciousness of the immediate present. All history, however, is contemporary history in this rigorous and precise sense; it is a condition of all history that it should live, be present in the mind of the historian; all history springs directly from present life, since only an interest of our present life can induce us to inquire into the past, which, by being made history, is no longer a past but a present. If, Croce says, "contemporaneity is not the characteristic of one class of histories (as it is held to be, and with good reasons, in an empirical classification), but the intrinsic character of all history, the relation between history and life must be conceived of as a relation of unity:

not certainly in the sense of an abstract identity, but in that of a synthetic unity, which implies both the unity and the distinction of the terms. *T*o speak of a history, of which we do not possess the documents, will then seem as absurd as to speak of the existence of a certain thing, of which we should at the same time affirm that one of the essential conditions for its existence is lacking. A history without relation with the document would be an unverifiable history; and since the reality of history lies in this verifiability, and the historical narrative in which it realizes itself is an historical narrative only in so far as it is the critical exposition of the document, a history of that kind, without meaning and without truth, would be inexistent as history. How could ever a history of painting be composed by a man who should not see and enjoy the works of which he intends to describe critically the origin and development? How, a history of philosophy, without the works, or at least the fragments of the works of the philosophers? How, the history of a feeling or a custom, for instance, of Christian humility or of chivalresque honour, without the capacity to re-live, or rather, without actually re-living those particular states of mind? "On the other hand, having established the indissoluble connection of life and thought in history, the doubts that have been advanced about the certainty and utility of history suddenly and totally disappear, and it becomes almost impossible to understand them. How

could that ever be uncertain, which is a present product of our spirit?   How could a knowledge be useless, which solves a problem rising from the womb
of life?" [1]

If history is thus regarded not as an object but
as an activity, not as the irrevocable past but as
the living present, the difference between history
and chronicle, which is one of the puzzles of historical
thought, becomes an important and significant distinction.   We are used to think that the original
form of historical writing is the chronicle, and
history a later and maturer development.   Now
if history is the consciousness of a present, it follows that history is contemporary with the event;
that, therefore, the most meagre chronicle, in the
mind of its writer, moved by the actuality of the
facts which he records, is already a history in the
full sense of the word.   And the records of the
past, whether appearing to us, from a literary
point of view, as mere chronicles or as true
histories, become history again whenever they are
apprehended by a new mind as an answer to a
present problem, partaking of the activity of the
mind that thinks them anew.   The same records,
on the other hand, are a mere chronicle, an
empty narrative, a truly irrevocable past, whenever they are not re-lived by a living mind,
either because they do not correspond to any interest of present life, or because the essential con-

[1] *Teoria e Storia*, pp. 5–6.

ditions for the recreation of that past, the documents which enable us to revive within ourselves the original experience, are irrevocably lost. The true distinction between history and chronicle is not, therefore, a literary or material one, but a distinction between forms of spiritual activity: history is the living consciousness, and, therefore, an act of thought or knowledge; chronicle is the dead record, which we preserve by a mere act of will, because we know that some day the dead record itself may come back to life, transform itself again, under an impulse rooted not in the past but in the present, into a living thought.

"These revivals have purely inward motives; and no amount of narratives or documents can produce them; on the contrary, it is the inner motive that gathers and brings before itself documents and narratives, which, without it, would remain dispersed and inert. And it will be for ever impossible to understand the effectual process of historical thought, unless one starts from the principle that the spirit itself is history, and, in every one of its moments, the maker of history and at the same time the result of all foregoing history; so that the spirit carries within itself the whole of its history, which in fact coincides with the spirit itself. To forget one aspect of history and to remember another is nothing but the rhythm of the life of the spirit, which works by determining and individualizing itself, and by in-determining and dis-individualizing the preceding determinations and individualizations, in order to create new and richer ones. The spirit would live over again, so to speak, its history, even without those external objects which we call narratives and documents; but those external objects are instruments that it fashions for itself, and preparatory acts that it accomplishes, in order to effect that vital interior evocation, in whose process they resolve themselves. And for this purpose the spirit asserts and jealously preserves the 'memories of the past.'" [1]

This practical function of the preservation of the dead documents and records is the work of the pure scholar, of the erudite, the archivist, the archæologist, or what might be termed philology in the strict sense of the word. And it is a legitimate and useful function, provided that it does not pretend to be other than it actually is, and to substitute itself for the true process of history, by attempting to make history with the external objects that have been confided to its care. Philological histories are never anything but mere compilations, learned chronicles, useful repertories; and as such, blameless; but as histories they lack the living spirit, the creative impulse, which alone can transform the document into history. We have only to turn our attention to the greatest part of our modern histories of literature, whether written by a single philologist or by a learned society, to realize that

[1] *Teoria e Storia*, pp. 15–16.

that which is philology in them is not history, but
repertory; and the rest, which is history, is not
philology, but a vivid reaction, an act of present
life, by which some at least of the documents of the
past (since some philologists are men) have suddenly
become part of the actual experience of the writer,
answered his spiritual need, stirred that which is
still human in his soul. And if a further confirmation of the philological error is needed, and of the
further errors in which it involves the philological
historian, it is sufficient to open those same literary
histories at the pages in which they attempt to explain the origins of the Renaissance. Because as
those writers make history from the sources, so
they imagine that life itself springs from material
sources; and the Renaissance finds its *causes* in the
discovery of monuments and documents of the
classical world, in the lives and travels of humanists,
in the munificence of popes and princes. It does not
seem to occur to them that monuments and manu-
scripts, which materially had existed in Europe
during all the so-called Dark and Middle Ages,
could not have been discovered unless, at a certain
moment in the development of European civilization, the spirit of the Western nations had not
craved those particular helps to its own life, because
of motives and impulses generated by its own actual
experience; and that the mediæval *clericus* was not
less of a traveller than the humanist, and that the
economic aspect of life can never be intelligibly

conceived as a cause of that life of which it is but a moment. For the philological historian, the Renaissance begins between the end of the four-teenth and the beginning of the fifteenth century; but the historian *tout court* knows that the funda-mental impulses and motives by which we empiric-ally characterize that period in the history of the human spirit were already present in the Italy of the thirteenth century, and slowly maturing in the other European countries long before any of the Italian humanists had come to them as the apostles of a new creed.

If philological history is not history but pseudo-history, so are also two other forms of so-called historical thought, poetical history and rhetorical history. The first substitutes for the value of history, which is thought, a purely immediate and senti-mental, or æsthetic value; it presents itself very often as a reaction to philological history, but it falls into the opposite error, which is that of putting the imagination in the place of the document. Rhetorical history is that which is animated by practical ends (moralistic, nationalistic, or other), and it really consists of two distinct elements, history itself, and the particular end towards which the recitation of history is directed, converging into a single practical act. Both partake of life much more intensely than philological history; but the life of the one is poetry, that of the other is economic or moral action. They are, therefore, legitimate as poetry and as action, and become errors only in so far as they are presented as history. It is important to make this distinction as clear as possible: the actual interest which makes history is not for Croce a sentimental or practical interest, but an interest of thought. In the distinction of the various forms of spiritual activity, history is not the sentimental or practical moment, but the moment of ultimate consciousness, the reflection and not either the intuition or the action, the thought which is consciousness of life and not life immediate; neither art nor morality, in a word, but philosophy, if by philosophy, we mean not a formal discipline, but all knowledge *sub specie universalis*. The defenders of rhetorical history have become more frequent during and after the war than they were before it, it being only too natural that in times of exceptional stress truth should be made subservient to practical ends, and the man of knowledge should be unwittingly transmogrified into a man of action; and they insist more than ever on the moral efficacy of history as its proper educational value. But "if by history we mean both that history which is thought, and those that are poetry, philology or moral will, it is clear that 'history' will enter into the educational process not under one only, but under all these forms; though as history proper, under one only, which is not that of moral education, exclusively and abstractly considered, but of the education or development of thought." [1]

[1] *Teoria e Storia*, pp. 35–6.

The conception of history as contemporary history, or present thought, helps us to discard that form of historical scepticism, or agnosticism, which affirms that all we can know of history is but one part, and a very small part, of the whole. If we should imagine that infinite whole, in its infinite detail, as present for one moment to our mind, all we could do, would be instantly to proceed to forget it, in order to concentrate our attention on that detail only which answers to a problem and, therefore, constitutes a living and active history. That whole is not something of which we can affirm the existence at any given moment, but the eternal phantasm of the thing in itself, the limiting concept of the infinity of our doing and knowing: a naturalistic construction similar to the external and material reality of physical science. It is this naturalistic process that gives birth to agnosticism, in history as in science; that is, to the affirmation of the impossibility of knowing that which has no reality outside our own thought, which has created, or rather posited it, for its own purposes. A further consequence is that we must renounce the knowledge of universal history, not as a fact, because as such it has never existed, but as a pretence under which, in fact, we are given something quite different. The pretence consists (and it will be well to recall Croce's own words, written long before some recent attempts, which in those words find their precise valuation) in "reducing within a single frame all the facts of mankind, from its origins on earth to the present day; or rather, since in this way history would not be truly universal, from the origins of things or from the Creation to the end of the world; hence a tendency to fill the abysm of prehistory or of the origins with theological or naturalistic novels, and somehow to outline the future, either with revelations or with prophecies, as in the Christian universal history (which extended to the Anti-Christ and to the universal judgment), or with forecasts, as in the universal histories of positivism, democraticism, and socialism. Such is the pretence; but the fact turns out to be different from the intention, and what we get is either a more or less heterogeneous chronicle, or a poetical history expressing some aspiration of the heart, or even a true history, which is not universal but particular, though embracing the life of many nations and of many epochs; and, more often, in the same literary body we discern these divers elements, one by the side of the other." [1]

Universal history is a utopian ideal similar to those of a universal language, or of universal art, or of a law that should be valid for all times; the only useful meaning of the word universal when applied to history is that of a recommendation to enlarge the sphere of our historical interests, and to turn from the knowledge of one time and one people to that of the great facts and currents of history. But a denial

[1] *Teoria e Storia*, p. 46.

of the validity of universal history must not be understood as withdrawing from history the knowledge of the universal. The reader who has followed us through the preceding chapters, and especially through our analysis of the historical judgment, knows how the concreteness and individuality of history is determined by thought, and therefore known as a universal. History is thought, and, as such, the thought of the universal in its concrete and particular determinations. The object of history is never this or that poet, but poetry; not this or that nation or epoch, but culture, civilization, progress, freedom, or a similar word which denotes the development of the human spirit as a whole, and is therefore a universal. It is of history, thus conceived, of contemporary history, as opposed to the naturalistic moment (chronicle, or philological history), that Croce asserts the identity with philosophy. history as the knowledge of the eternal present being one with the thought of the eternal present, which is philosophy. History renounces the pretence of an objective universality in the same way as philosophy, immanent in and identical with history, abolishes the idea of a universal philosophy: the two negations are but one, since the closed system, the final truth, is as much a cosmological novel as universal history is. "This tendency was implicit in Hegel's philosophy, but contrasted within it by old prejudices, and wholly betrayed in the execution, so that even that philosophy converted itself into a cosmological novel;

we can therefore say that that which at the beginning of the nineteenth century was a mere presentiment, only at the beginning of the twentieth is transforming itself into a firm consciousness, which defies the fears of the timid, that in this way we endanger the knowledge of the universal; maintaining that, on the contrary, in this way only this knowledge is obtained truly and for ever, because in a dynamic mode. History becoming actual history, and philosophy becoming historical philosophy, have freed themselves, one from the dread of not being able to know that which is not known only because either it was or it will be known, and the other, from the despair of never attaining the final truth: that is, both have freed themselves from the phantasm of the 'thing in itself.'" [1]

This final affirmation of the unity of human thought, this qualification of all thought as at the same time historical and philosophical, is the last answer given by Croce to the problem which had occupied him for the last twenty years, ever since his first speculations on history as art. From the consideration of the individual moment which is essential to history, he had slowly raised himself to the contemplation of the pure universal, only to return finally to the individual moment in which only the universal realizes itself. And while this answer can be regarded, on the whole, as the natural conclusion of the idealistic movement in philosophy, yet it dif-

[1] *Teoria e Storia*, pp. 51-2.

fers from Kant in its ultimate repudiation of the *noumenon*, from Hegel, in that it makes it impossible to build, side by side with a dynamic logic, a my- thology of the Idea, a philosophy of history and of nature, in which the transcendental element, elimi- nated already from the logic, should find its ultimate refuge. It is to be hoped that Croce's critics will not level against him those same criticisms that are generally employed against Kant or Hegel, because they would be for the most part ineffectual against a Kantian and Hegelian philosopher who has dis- carded the whole of Kantian and Hegelian meta- physics. From this standpoint, Croce is not only the heir of the idealistic, but also of the positivistic or realistic tradition, which he has constantly opposed, not because of its antimetaphysical character, but because in the external reality of the realist, in the natural or historical philosophy of the positivist, he is unable to see anything but naturalistic disguises of the old metaphysical entities. A realist who should not in principle refuse to become acquainted with Croce's thought, but honestly attempt to understand it, would probably find his own realism purified and made more truly realistic by the experience.

A material distinction, as of formal disciplines, between history and philosophy still survives in Croce's theory, philosophy proper being considered as the categoric or methodological moment of his- tory—a distinction roughly corresponding to the one he made in his logic between the individual judgment

and the definition.   But philosophy itself is profoundly modified once we fully realize that its historical character implies the abandonment of certain
features which are constantly associated in our minds
with the idea of philosophy, because of its early
associations with mythology and the positive religions.   To these belong the belief in the existence of a
fundamental problem of philosophy, which remains
the same throughout the history of human thought,
and of which the various philosophies are but successive approximations to an answer; the consequent
stress laid on the unity of the system rather than on
the fine and clear distinctions; the research of an
ultimate truth; and finally, the prejudice by which
the philosopher is regarded as a Buddha or priest,
freed from human passions and human illusions,
resting in the pure contemplation of a truth, which,
by being torn from the soil of active life that has
borne it, cannot but wither away and become as
empty and unreal as the Buddha's own Nirvana
frankly professes to be.   Metaphysics to Croce is
the last incarnation of theology; and the professor of
philosophy in our universities, with a culture formed
exclusively on the books of the great philosophers of
the past, unmoved by the passions and problems
of life, is but the heir of the mediæval master of
theology.   "A strong advancement of philosophical
culture ought to tend towards this result: that all
the students of human things, jurists, economists,
moralists, men of letters, that is, all the students of

historical matters, should become conscious and well-disciplined philosophers; and the philosopher in general, the *purus philosophus*, should no longer find place among the professional specifications of knowledge." [1]

We shall not follow our author in all his developments of the theory of history. It suffices to say that these developments are obviously but new presentations, made here and there more precise and more coherent, of the various problems already discussed in the preceding volumes of the *Filosofia dello Spirito*. We shall thus recognise in Croce's criticism of the philosophy of history as a special discipline, distinct both from history as such and from a so-called general philosophy, his polemic against transcendence, either metaphysical or naturalistic; and in his claim for the positivity of history, his theory of value, by which the only real values are the positive ones, coinciding with the fact, while negative values are but expressions of feelings and desires. In the light of this theory, since history is obviously concerned with that which is, and not with that which is not, the limits of historical judgment are clearly established, in the way in which we saw them established for literary criticism. As the literary critic is never concerned with anything but with expression, or art, or beauty, non-expression, non-art, non-beauty being as such inexistent, and truly existent only as manifestations of the logical or practical activity of

[1] *Teoria e Storia*, p. 145.

man; so the historian at large will never meet negative values, but positive facts only, which assume the
aspect of ugliness, or error, or immorality, only in the
dialectic process of reality, in the creation of a higher
form of life. His affirmation of the positive fact is
sufficient judgment, and it becomes an implicit
moral judgment whenever the consciousness of the
historian is a moral consciousness, without any need
for him to usurp the function of the moralist or of the
judge in apportioning praise or blame on the objects
of his history.

Against the humanistic or pragmatic conception of
history, which finds the reasons and motives of history in the abstract individual, as against the opposite view, for which the true history is only that of
the collectivity, of the institutions, of the human
values, Croce reasserts his concept of the actuality of
the spirit, in regard to which the individual is as
much of an abstraction as the society or the value
which does not entirely realize itself in the fact. The
object of history is neither Pericles nor Politics,
neither Sophocles nor Tragedy, neither Plato nor
Philosophy; but the universal in the individual, that
is, Politics, Tragedy, Philosophy, as Pericles, Sophocles, and Plato, or Pericles, Sophocles, and Plato as
particular moments of Politics, of Tragedy, and of
Philosophy.

As there are no special philosophical sciences, and
then a general philosophy, which should be outside
or above them, but whenever we think of reality

under one of its aspects or distinctions, we think of
the whole of reality in one of its determinations, so
there are no special histories, the limits of which can
be definitely stated, and above them a general history, which would in a new form revive the myth of
universal history. We have seen how literary history,
for instance, tends inevitably to become the whole
spiritual history of a nation; and the same applies to
all special histories, whether political or moral, or
philosophical. There are divisions of history, according to the quality of the objects, to time and
space, but such divisions are mere empirical classifications, practical instruments or literary expedients;
and we can use as the foundation of such divisions
even the ideal distinctions of the fundamental forms
of spiritual activity. But when these distinctions are
understood as actual distinctions of the aspects of the
spiritual life, of which we make history, then all the
other aspects will inevitably be present in the particular distinction, once we truly apprehend it in the
fulness of its relations. In this sense, history is always special or particular, because it is only in the
special and particular that we can grasp the effectual
and concrete universality, the effectual and concrete
unity.

Finally, the difference between the history of man
and the history of nature is not a difference in the
object but in the method of history. The whole of
reality is spiritual reality, and nature apprehended in
its concreteness and actuality, if we are able to re-

create it within ourselves, becomes actual, concrete, contemporary history as much as any part of human history. On the other hand, the application of empirical and abstract concepts, the practical manipulation of the data of human history, transforms the history of man into mere natural history. This difference in method we have already analyzed in studying Croce's logic, and we shall only add here that the reader of Croce may often be tempted to regard Croce's conception of reality as limited to the human spirit only, and therefore to give a metaphysical interpretation to his exclusion of "nature." The correct interpretation is a purely epistemological one, and again and again Croce insists that in the whole of reality, which is development or life, man and nature are but empirical and abstract distinctions. On the other hand, Croce's interests are certainly more human than natural, and not only in the sense in which this is true of every man; in the more precise sense also that the effort to recreate within himself the consciousness of a blade of grass, which he advises the historian of nature to perform, clearly appeals to him so little, that he may even seem doubtful of its success. The accent is continually laid, in Croce's thought, on the history of man, and on the thought of man; to many of us, our dealings with nature (not the dead nature of Linnæus, but the living nature of Virgil and Shelley) would probably suggest a shifting of the accent by which the spirituality of nature, the continuity of the dynamic process from nature to man would become more emphatically affirmed than it is in any of Croce's writings. We are probably touching here on one of the possible, and probable, lines of development of Croce's philosophy; which, however, will not become actual until the historical problems of the living nature shall not urge Croce himself, or one of his successors, as powerfully as the problems of human history have moved him. At present, with very rare exceptions, the students of the history of nature are occupied in transforming their historical experience into classes and types and laws; but a time may come when from the naturalistic constructions we shall be able more frequently to recreate the life of which these are but the dead spoils, the accumulated vestiges, by the same process by which history rekindles the old chronicles into new, contemporary life. That such a development is implied in Croce's own theory of history can hardly be questioned, though, when realized, it will undoubtedly react on more than one point of Croce's logic.

III. CRITICISM AND HISTORY

Beyond the system—The universality of art—The discipline of art—Poetry, prose and oratory—Classicism and impressionism—Practical personality and poetical personality—The monographic method in criticism—The reform of æsthetic history—Criticism as philosophy—Sensibility and intelligence.

THE identification of history and philosophy, in the form in which we have expounded it in the preceding chapter, is the turning point of Croce's thought; the system which in the first three volumes of the *Filosofia dello Spirito* had still a somewhat static and rigid appearance, is really set to movement, animated as if by a new and intenser life, since its implicit dynamism is made explicit in the fourth and concluding volume. To Croce himself, the whole of his work appears no longer as a system, but as "a series of systematizations," and his *Filosofia dello Spirito*, as a series of "volumes on the problems slowly gathering in his mind since the years of his youth." No wonder, therefore, that his later work should contain "thoughts that break the bars of the so-called system, and give, to a close scrutiny, new systems or new 'systematizations,' since always the whole moves with every one of our steps." No wonder that he should feel that he will continue to philosophize even if one day he shall abandon "philosophy," "as this is what the unity of philosophy and history implies: that we philosophize whenever we think, and of whatever object and in whatever form we may think." [1] And in fact, in these last few years, Croce has given many a severe shock to the faithful worshippers of his system, sometimes by extending his tolerance, or even his approval, to types of speculation apparently remote from his own, but in which he recognises, under a radically different aspect, some of the living impulses, and spiritual interests by which his own thought is moved; and sometimes by developing new theories, through which intellectual positions criticised by him at an earlier stage of his work were reëstablished as having a new meaning and value, once they were approached from a new and higher standpoint, partly reached by means of that same critical process which had previously revealed them as errors. Croce's conception of the function of error in the history of human thought, while making him violently intolerant of actual negative error, leads him to search painstakingly for that element of truth which is the reality of every error; and in this respect too, his philosophical career is as it were roughly divided into two periods, one of critical dissolution, and the other of critical reconstruction, respectively corresponding to the building up of the system, and to the successive liberation from the shackles of the system itself. Croce's name will certainly be remembered in the future, if on no

[1] *Contributo,* pp. 79–81.

other account, as that of the only philosopher who never became the slave of his dead thought. His coherence is never of the letter, but of the spirit.

This last phase of Croce's thought offers greater difficulties to the expositor than the preceding ones, partly because it is still in the making, and therefore lacks the necessary perspective, and partly because it is embodied not only in purely philosophical essays, but in every page of Croce's historical and critical writings; so that very often it would be impossible to give a clear account of it without ample and minute reference to the underlying historical material. The whole of Croce's thought could indeed be restated through an exposition of Croce's historical views, and it would be an alluring task to extract from his writings a kind of outline of the history of mankind, considered especially in its aesthetic and philosophical manifestations, and indirectly also in its moral and economic activities; but it would take us much beyond the limits which we have set to our labour. We shall therefore confine ourselves to examining, in this chapter, the latest developments of Croce's æsthetics, especially in relation with the history of art and poetry; and, in the following and concluding one, to considering his theory of truth or of the function of thought, in relation to other types of contemporary thought.

We have followed the evolution, or rather the deepening, of Croce's concept of art as pure intuition, into lyrical intuition, through which the move-

ment and life which might seem to have been denied
to the products of the æsthetic activity considered
as a mere form of knowledge, were recognised as
intrinsically belonging to them by reason of the
very nature of that cognitive activity, and of its
relations with the practical sphere of the spirit,
the states of mind, which can be abstracted as the
matter or content of the æsthetic form. Another
difficulty, however, still persisted in Croce's theory,
due to the sharp distinction between the æsthetic
and the logical activity, which reserved to the first
the field of individual, to the second that of universal
knowledge—constituting a double-grade relation,
in which the æsthetic was implied by the logic
activity, but not vice-versa. The corresponding
distinction of the two forms of the practical spirit,
the economic and the ethic, evolved by Croce
at a maturer stage of his speculation, establishes
not only a double-grade relation, but also a re-
ciprocal implication. Croce's essay on *Il carattere
di totalità della espressione artistica* (1917) is an
attempt at interpreting his first distinction in the
light of the second, thereby recognising the universal or *cosmic* character of art. That universality
which becomes explicit in the logical judgment is
implicit in the intuition, already identified with
the category of feeling, with the concrete states
of mind, on which it imposes its form: "Since, what
is a feeling or a state of mind? is it something that
can be detached from the universe and developed

by itself? have the part and the whole, the individual and the cosmos, the finite and the infinite, any reality, one outside the other? One may be inclined to grant that every severance and isolation of the two terms of the relation could not be anything but the work of abstraction, for which only there is an abstract individuality and an abstract finite, an abstract unity and an abstract infinite. But the pure intuition, or artistic representation, abhors abstraction; or rather it does not even abhor it, since it knows it not, because of its naïve or auroral cognitive character. In it, the individual lives by the life of the whole, and the whole is in the life of the individual; and every true artistic representation is itself and the universe, the universe in that individual form, and that individual form as the universe. In every accent of a poet, in every creature of his phantasy, there is the whole of human destiny, all the hopes, the illusions, the sorrows and the joys, all human greatness and all human misery, the entire drama of reality, which perpetually becomes and grows upon itself, suffering and rejoicing." [1]

This recognition of the implicit universality of the æsthetic expression does not abolish, as it might seem to a superficial observer, the distinction between æsthetic and logical knowledge; it rather makes it clearer and truer. An imperfect recognition may lead to an intellectualistic or mystic theory

[1] *Nuovi Saggi, di Estetica,* p. 126.

of art; and intellectualism and mysticism in æsthetics remain for Croce as typical forms of error,
whether they are directed towards a confusion
between intuition and judgment, or towards a
symbolical or allegorical interpretation of art, or
towards a semi-religious theory of art as the revelation of the *Deus absconditus.* But the truth that
those errors tried to express in their imperfect formulas, is finally understood by him to be that character of universality which belongs to every aspect
and to every fragment of the living reality. Feeling
itself, or a state of mind, partakes in its actuality
of that universal character, but when expressed in
art, it retains its universality only by losing its praetical nature, and subjecting itself entirely to the form
which expresses it. Thus the æsthetic activity,
because bent on realizing its own universality,
which is the perfection of its form, imposes on the
artist a morality and a discipline which cannot be
identified with practical morality, with the discipline
of life. The sincerity of the artist is of another
order than that of the practical man, though (we
can never repeat it too often) æsthetic virtues being
incommensurable with moral values, his work as an
artist does not exempt him from his duties as a man.

This further determination of the concept of
expression is used by Croce to clarify a distinction
which had already been adumbrated in the *Estetica;*
the distinction between poetic, intellectual, and
practical expression, between the word in which

the pure intuition embodies itself, the word which
is a sign or symbol of thought, and the word which
is an instrument for the awakening of the emotions,
a preparation for action. Thus the old categories
of poetry, prose, and oratory reappear, but no longer
as criteria of material classification, no longer to be
identified with classes or genres of expression. They
become synonyms, respectively, of the æsthetic,
the logical, and the practical activity; to be used
as instruments of literary and artistic criticism, if
the critic is willing to renounce all external helps
and material standards, and to penetrate into the
"individuality of the act, where only it is given to
him to discern the different spiritual dispositions,
and what is poetry from what is not poetry. Under
the semblance of prose, in a comedy or in a novel,
we may find a true and deeply felt lyric; as under
that of verse, in a tragedy or in a poem, nothing but
reflection and oratory."[1] It is easy to perceive
how this distinction will also react on Croce's theory
of language as intuition and expression, not by
altering its initial position, but by offering new
means for the empirical analysis of the facts of
language, the nature of which is obviously determined by the kind of impulse which man obeys
in the individual act of expression. By the employment of such a method, the history of language
as æsthetic expression can be qualified and illum-
ined through the consideration of the moments

[1] *Nuovi Saggi*, p. 142. Also *Conversazioni Critiche*, I, pp. 58-63.

in which language ceases to be a pure act of æsthetic creation, and is subordinated, as a symbol or
instrument, to the purposes of the logical and
practical mind.

Similarly, in the history of poetry or of art, the
consideration of the logical and practical moments
in the expression will help to define and isolate
that which is purely æsthetic expression, that is,
poetry and art. Croce's expressionistic theory,
when thus understood, differs both from other
expressionistic theories and from the narrow interpretations of Croce's own theory that have been
given by some of his followers and by all his adversaries. It does not, in fact, attempt to give an
æsthetic justification of art as the mere passive
reception of the transient mood; it has no sympathy
for that impressionism which transforms the artist
into a reed shaken by all winds of circumstance,
legitimizing every intrusion of the practical personality in the æsthetic production. It reduces
this modern æsthetics of the immediate feeling
to an expression, not of the true spirit of what art
and poetry is being produced to-day, but of that
disease, or passivity, of the times, the first solemn
document of which can be traced in Rousseau's
Confessions. Against it, Croce appeals to the example and the word of a Goethe or a Leopardi,
who diagnosed the disease in its inception, and
contrasted the classical naturalness and simplicity
of the ancients with the affectation and tumidity

of the moderns. But the classicism which Croce
invokes is not a formal and literal ideal, limited to
certain models or standards: it is that complete
idealization, which the immediate practical data,
in all times and climates, will undergo at the hands
of the true poet and artist, whether he calls himself
a romanticist or a classicist, an idealist or a realist.

Closely related with this line of thought is Croce's
distinction of the practical from the poetical personality of the artist, and of biography from æsthetic
criticism, as we find it in the essay of *Alcune massime
critiche,* and in the first chapter of his study on
Shakespeare (1919). The knowledge of the facts
of an artist's life is undoubtedly required for the
purposes of biographical or practical history; but
their relation with the æsthetic personality of the
artist is not, as it is generally assumed, a relation
of cause and effect. They may have an indirect
utility for the definition of the æsthetic personality,
and especially for the recognition of that which in
the works of art themselves is still purely practical,
not yet stamped with the seal of the æsthetic activity.
But in the apprehension of art, the critic must
prescind from the biographical elements, because
"the artist himself has prescinded from them in
the act of creation of his work of art, which is a
work of art inasmuch as it is the opposite of the
practical life, and is accomplished by the artist
raising himself above the practical plane, abandoning the greatest part of his practical feelings, and

transfiguring those even that he seems to preserve, because putting them into new relations. The artist, as we say, 'transcends time,' that is, the 'practical time,' and enters the 'ideal time,' where actions do not follow actions, but the eternal lives in the present. And he who pretends to explain the ideal time by the practical time, the imaginative creation by the practical action, art by biography, unwittingly denies art itself, and reduces it to a practical business, of the same kind as eating and making love, producing goods or fighting for a political cause." [1]

This concept of the æsthetic personality, which we find clearly defined in Croce's most recent essays, was the guiding principle of all his literary criticism, since the time when he started his series of studies on modern Italian literature. He had inherited it from De Sanctis, whose work, in so far as it is æsthetic and not moral or political history, can be regarded as a collection of powerful characterizations of aesthetic personalities. But, in his first attempts in literary criticism, Croce employed it tentatively in what then appeared to him only as the preparatory stage of his work; beyond the individual characterizations, and once these had been sufficiently determined, he still thought of the possibility of a general literary history, in which these should find their place as parts of a more complex organism of critical thought. But

[1] *Nuovi Saggi*, p. 231.

when he had completed his task, in a series of remarkable essays, some of which will have fixed for
a long time to come the physiognomy of the most
notable Italian writers of the last half-century, he
perceived that he had practically exhausted the
æsthetic problems which the work of those writers
presented to his mind: a general literary history
of the period could have been nothing but a new
arrangement of the same ideas and valuations
contained in the individual essays. Thus the monographic method which he had originally adopted
for convenience' sake, justified itself in the practice
of his work, or rather proved to be the only legitimate method of literary and general artistic history. All the vague abstractions with which modern
nationalistic or sociological histories of art and poetry are crammed, reveal themselves ultimately
as either generalizations of individual characteristics, or concepts borrowed from the economic
and moral history of a nation or people, more or
less irrelevant to the purposes of æsthetic criticism.
The true unity in the consideration of the history of
art cannot be reached by the establishment of purely
external and material relations between work and
work, between artist and artist, but only by making
one's critical estimate of the individual work or
artist sufficiently vast and sufficiently deep. "Contemporaries, related or opposed to the individual
poet, his more or less partial and remote forerunners,
the moral and intellectual life of his time, and that

of the times which preceded and prepared it, these and other things are all present (now expressed, now unexpressed) in our spirit, when we reconstruct the dialectic of a given artistic personality. Undoubtedly, in considering a given personality we cannot, in the same act, consider another or many others or all others, each for itself; and psychologists call this lack of ubiquity the 'narrowness of the threshold of consciousness,' while they ought to call it the highest energy of the human spirit, which sinks itself in the object that in a given moment interests it, and does not allow itself under any condition to be diverted from it, because in the individual it finds all that interests it, and, in a word, the Whole." [1]

This is the purport of the essay on *La Riforma della Storia artistica e letteraria* (1917), and this is the method deliberately followed by Croce in his recent essays on Ariosto, Goethe, Shakespeare, Corneille and Dante, which ought to be studied not only as characterizations of the various poets, of the feeling or tonality which is peculiar to each of them and constitutes their æsthetic personality, but also as sources for the methodology of literary criticism. To his theory Croce brings a two-fold corroboration, first, from the observation of the fact that it coincides with a more and more wide-spread tendency in both literary and artistic history towards the monographic form, the individual essay,

[1] *Nuovi Saggi,* p. 181.

as the most effectual type of criticism; and second, from the analogy with other forms of history. All history, and not æsthetic history only, is essentially monographic; all history is the history of a given event or of a given custom or of a given doctrine, and all history reaches the universal only in and through the individual. The only obstacles to a general acceptation of this view are, on one side, a persistent inability to distinguish art from the practical and moral life and from philosophy, and on the other, a lack of scientific sense, through which science is regarded not as critical research, but as a material gathering of facts. Prospectuses, handbooks, dictionaries and encyclopedias are not the ideal of history: they are instruments of which we shall always make use as practical helps for the critical research; but what is living and real thought in them is but an echo of the actual thinking of individual problems.

All æsthetic criticism, and therefore all æsthetic history, is this thinking of logical problems, rooted in the concrete ground of the works of art, which are in their turn solutions of æsthetic problems. For this the dynamic conception of the human spirit imports that every one of its acts is a creation, or a *doing*, in the particular form in which the spirit realizes itself; art, a creation, in respect to which all spiritual antecedents assume the aspect of a given æsthetic problem; history or philosophy, a creation on the substance of reality presenting itself as a logical problem; and the whole sphere of the theo-

retical spirit, "a theoretical *doing*, which is the perpetual antecedent and the perpetual consequent
of the practical doing." [1] *T*he mere recreation of
the æsthetic impression given by a work of art is
not yet criticism; the critic as a mere *artifex additus
artifici* is not yet a critic, but still an artist. Criticism, like all other history, is not feeling or intuition,
but intelligence and thought. Every history of
criticism will therefore ultimately coincide with
the history of æsthetic theories, with the philosophy
of art.

We thus reach again, by a new path, the identification of history with philosophy; to which, in this
particular case, the most common objection is that
what is required in a critic is much more an exquisite
æsthetic sensibility than an elaborate concept of
what art is as a category of the human mind. But
the objection rests on a misunderstanding of the
proper function of criticism. What sensibility can
give is but the immediate apprehension or taste
of the work of art, critically dumb in itself; on the
other hand, it is impossible to conceive of a true
intelligence of art, "without the conjoined capacity
to understand the individual works of art, because
philosophy does not develop in the abstract, but
is stimulated by the acts of life and imagination,
rises for the purpose of comprehending them, and
understands them by understanding itself." [2] *T*he

---

[1] *L'arte come Creazione* (1918), in *Nuovi Saggi*, p. 160.
[2] *La Critica Letteraria come Filosofia* (1918), in *Nuovi Saggi*, p. 217.

mere æsthetic sensibility makes but a new artist;
what makes the critic is his philosophy. Here also,
however, as during the whole course of our inquiry,
we must not identify philosophy with the official
history of philosophical disciplines, which offers a
large number of theories of æsthetics only remotely
related to the concrete works of art, to the concrete
processes of æsthetic creation, but with the whole
history of human thought, with the working out
of particular problems successively presented to
the intelligence of man by the actual developments
of poetry and art.   The æsthetic judgment, like
every other judgment, is a synthesis of the individual
intuition, or subject, and of the universal category,
or predicate; and this is but another way of stating
the identity of æsthetic criticism, as of all forms
of history, with philosophy. The critic must be
endowed with a power to give new life, within his
own mind, to the intuitions of the artist, but this
is for him but the soil in which his thought must
spread its roots; it is true that without that power,
no criticism is possible, but it is equally true that
no philosophy of art can grow on any but that same
soil.   The ultimate test of the validity of æsthetic
thought is in its capacity to expand our sphere of
æsthetic apprehension; and pure æsthetics is but
the methodological moment of æsthetic history or
criticism.

IV. VERITAS FILIA TEMPORIS

Quid est veritas?—Platonism, or transcendental idealism—Naturalism, or transcendental realism—The idea of progress—Progress and truth: evolutionism—Pragmatism—Croce's new pragmatism—The immanence of value—The actuality of Truth—Truth as history: the function of error and of evil—The foundations of Croce's thought.

THERE is one problem in the history of human thought, which, however conscious we might be of the multiplicity and historical contingency of philosophical problems, yet can appear to us as the ultimate or central one, if only because it is an abstract interrogation describing the attitude of the philosopher, and to which every concrete logical research, every act of thought, can be reduced. It is Pilate's question: *Quid est veritas?* What is truth?

The question itself has no definite meaning, until it receives from the individual thinker a definite content, which is history or experience, and the infinite variety of the answers it has received is due to the infinite variability of that content. But at all times man has been urged by a passionate desire to lift his own individual answer from the flux of life, to put it as it were over and against that experience from which it had emerged, not as *the* truth of his particular problem, but as an abstractly universal truth. It is by violently breaking the process of thought, and hypostatizing in essence the subject of his thought, abstracted from its object, or the object from its subject, and both from the creative activity which produces truth, that man has created, both in philosophy proper and in the minds of the multitude, a double transcendence, of pure ideas, on one side, of brute matter on the other, from which the two most common meanings of the word truth are derived.

The Platonic idealist, for whom the actual processes of life and thought are but shadows and remembrances of the Eternal Ideas in the hyper-uranian space, can be assumed here as the symbol of the transcendental idealist, for whom truth is adequation to an ideal model existing outside the mind. The most disparate types of philosophers belong to this herd, and among them many that commonly go under the name of realists, since the idealist who has fixed and objectified his ideas cannot help considering them as real essences, and dealing with them accordingly. The Aristotelian realist, the theologian, Hegel himself when postulating an original Logos, of which Spirit and Nature are the temporal explication, all can be gathered together in the goodly company of Platonists; and Platonists are to-day both the literal followers of German idealism, and the less barbarous among contemporary realists, who are in the habit of attributing an independent, absolute existence to logical or mathematical abstractions. But neither the ones nor the others seem to be in very close contact with the spirit of the age: what they mean by truth is not what is generally meant by truth to-day, except among those who still cling to the myths in which that form of transcendence expressed itself in past ages. The sturdiest, though hardly recognizable, survivals of Platonism are relics of formalistic logic, still very frequent in contemporary culture, and a belief in what might be called average truth, mechanically extracted from an external and material consensus of opinions. But with this conception of truth, we touch the border line between idealistic and naturalistic transcendentalism.

The most common attitude of contemporary thought (and the one that is therefore usually designated as common sense, and as such opposed to philosophy) is a naïvely naturalistic one. But it would be a mistake to regard it as a simple and spontaneous attitude, and to identify it, for instance, with the naïve intuition of the artist, with a first grade of knowledge as yet untroubled by logical problems. The artist's vision is more distant from naturalism than the philosopher's concept, since common sense, however unreflected and illogical, is in itself a philosophy, and, though it may sound paradoxical, a transcendental one. The artist constantly identifies himself with his object; in his consciousness, the distinction between subject and object has not yet arisen. But the naïve naturalism

of which we are now speaking is posterior to the
logical judgment, in which that distinction first
appears; and is obtained by keeping separate the
two terms of the judgment, each of which exists
only in relation to the other, and by transforming
that relation into a quality of the object. The unity
thus disrupted is artificially reconstituted by abolish-
ing the subject, that is, by treating the subject itself
as merely an object among many objects, or as a
mere abstract intersection of objects. It is with
this form of naturalism that realism generally
coincides, and its abstracting process is the one that
has been recently systematized by the New Realists.
The justification of the naturalistic conception of
truth, as truth of description, and the motive of
its present popularity, is that it rests on a method
of knowledge which is indispensable to the natural
and mathematical sciences, and that the sciences
have come to usurp, in modern times, for reasons
which are obvious to every one, the place of science.
It is not the less true, however, that wherever that
method is applied, it reduces the living reality of
life and thought to a heap of dead, immovable
abstractions. There is no real danger in this as
long as the abstractions are taken for what they are,
and used as instruments for the purposes of our
doing and understanding; but when they are considered as a complete equivalent of the living reality,
then we become their prisoners, and are shut out
by them from all possibility of true understanding.

It is especially from the misuses of this method in the historical and moral sciences, from the degenerations of sociology, psychology, and philology, that we must be constantly on guard; lest in the very sciences of the human spirit we should miss that which is their true object, the human activity which creates the world of history and the values of life.

Modern thought, at the end of the Renaissance, begins with an attempt at eliminating that static conception of truth, in which both Platonism and naturalism find the roots of their transcendence. This is the origin of the idea of Progress, first established by Bruno, by Bacon, by Pascal, by Vico, in the form of a correlation between truth and time. Mediæval thought had been shackled for centuries by the authority of the ancients; the new thinkers invoked the authority of antiquity, of old age, and, therefore, of wisdom, not for the distant ages, in which the world could be said to be still young and inexperienced, but for their own times, in which it was possible to add a perpetually new experience and thought to that which had been bequeathed by the thinkers of Greece and Rome. The consequence of this attitude was the discovery of the immanence of truth in life, the liberation from the principle of authority (which had been the characteristic mediæval form of transcendence), and a vigorous impulse towards the recognition of the dynamic nature of reality, of what an American philosopher called the continuity of the ideal with the real. The thought that was contained in germ in those early polemics, vaguely and mythically in Bruno, and much more consciously in Vico, is substantially that of Croce's identification of philosophy with history.

We do not expect of a new philosophy that it should suddenly, as a revelation or illumination, give us a key to all the problems of reality, and resolve, once and forever, the so-called mystery of the universe. If such a thing should ever happen, it would mean the end of life, which cannot be conceived, in its ultimate essence, otherwise than as a perpetual positing and solution of problems. It must not be forgotten that a philosophy is the work of one man, and, therefore, contains only the answers to the problems that are real to him. But if we stop to consider the whole course of thought in the last two centuries, we shall realize that the idea of Progress, in many different and even in contrasting forms, is the one around which all our life, theoretical and practical, has centred in modern times. And of that idea, Croce's philosophy is the most powerful and coherent expression that has ever appeared. It is only by considering the whole of reality as activity, and the values of reality as coinciding with the forms of that activity, that Progress acquires a definite meaning: a progress which should be a constant approximation towards a preëxistent ideal, or a material process external to ourselves, would be a purely illusory one. In one case, our whole life would tend towards making a duplicate of that which already is—a work, therefore, without intrinsic worth, and without a real end; in the other, there would be no work at all, no activity, no life.

But nothing seems more difficult to our mind than to keep together the two ideas of progress and of truth. The natural sciences have made a gallant attempt at assimilating the idea of progress, and at transforming themselves, ultimately, into history. But the static concepts of naturalism resist that assimilation, and scientific evolutionism offers but the mechanical outline, the external processes of progress, the evolved and not the evolving reality; that is, it keeps its truth at the expense of its progress. This same evolutionism, when applied to the human sciences, is obviously unable to grasp the actuality of spiritual growth and life, and it only reproduces, in aggravated form, the evils inherent in all naturalistic interpretations of the spirit. Bergson's philosophy is a new evolutionism, which succeeds much better than the old one in retaining the idea of progress, and is, therefore, a further step towards the transformation of science into history; but what it gains in this respect, it loses in relation to its principle of truth, which is mythically represented as the lowest form of consciousness, or rather as that which is below consciousness itself.

What is vital in Bergson is his criticism of the

scientific, or naturalistic, intellect; but the intellect of man has other functions besides those of dissecting and classifying. From a similar beginning, that is, from the economic theory of science, derives another attempt at conciliating progress and truth, pragmatism. In pragmatism also, the critical element is more or less sound, but the constructive one is weak and arbitrary. Pragmatism does not reject the truth of science, because of its practical character; on the contrary, having recognized that the foundation of scientific truth is economic, it proceeds to deduce all truth from the will, and to verify it in action. The result of this deduction is a closer connection between truth and life than has been ever reached by any system of philosophy; but a merely apparent one, since truth itself is thus submerged and annulled in the immediacy of praetical and passional life. The solution of the problem of truth is obtained only by putting truth out of the question at the beginning of the inquiry; as it is clear that for a rigid pragmatist, there is but one truth left, and that is the truth of his theory, which, however, cannot be verified by the theory itself, since its usefulness is, to say the least, very doubtful.

By some of his adversaries Croce himself has been classed as a pragmatist. It is no wonder that certain distinctions should escape the attention of men who live to-day as exiles from distant centuries, and whose critical sight is, therefore, not clearer then that of an owl fluttering in the noonday sun.

But the only relation that I can think of between Croce and the pragmatists is that he advocates an economic theory not of truth, but of error; that he finds in the passions and practical interests of men the root of intellectual error. The problem of the positive relations between life and thought has been treated by him, as we know, in a very different spirit from that of the pragmatists; and in the circle of the human spirit, the ideal precedence is given by him, not to the practical but to the theoretical. On the other hand, in the actual process of time, all forms of human activity are reciprocally conditioned, and under this respect Croce's thought can be called, and has been called by himself, a new pragmatism, but "of a kind of which pragmatists have never thought, or at least which they have never been able to discern from the others, and to bring out in full relief. If life conditions thought, we have in this fact the clearly established demonstration of the always historically conditioned form of every thought: and not of art only, which is always the art of a time, of a soul, of a moment, but of philosophy also, which can solve but the problems that life proposes. Every philosophy reflects, and cannot help reflecting, the preoccupations, as they are called, of a determined historical moment; not, however, in the quality of its solutions (because in this case it would be a bad philosophy, a partisan or passional philosophy), but in the quality of its problems. And because the problem is historical, and the solution eternal, philosophy is at the same time contingent and eternal, mortal and immortal, temporary and extratemporary." [1]

Croce's conception of truth *is* his philosophy, and it is not my intention to summarize here what this book presents in what is already so rapid a survey. I wish only to point again at those doctrines of his, through which progress and truth are reconciled, without any sacrifice of the one to the other. Truth is for Croce a universal value or category of consciousness: its absoluteness rests on its character of universality, but, as a universal has no real being outside its concrete actuality, truth is nowhere if not in the individual judgment, that is, in the mind that creates it. It is strange that this mode of its manifestation should be considered to impair the quality of truth, while a similar objection would hardly be raised to-day in regard to other forms of spiritual activity. That the Beautiful is the value of the concrete, historical productions of the æsthetic spirit, or the Good that of the concrete, historically determined moral activity, these are concepts common to all contemporary thought, though no one, perhaps, has as yet expressed them as clearly as Croce. To the artist or to the saint, reality appears at a given moment as an æsthetic or an ethical problem; the terms of the problem are always particular, contingent, historical; yet when the artist or the saint

[1] *Filosofia della Pratica*, p. 208.

impresses on that reality the seal of his own deepest personality, when he creatively reacts to it, then the Beautiful and the Good realize themselves, as universal values, in the individual work of art or of mercy. Our belief in the absoluteness of the æsthetic or of the moral value is not weakened but strengthened by our inability to fix them in formulas or codes or standards; we see them perpetually transcending the reality in which they express themselves, by the same process by which that reality, which is all growth and life, transcends itself in the infinite course of its realization. We cannot think of any number of works of art or of mercy as exhausting the categories of the Beautiful or of the Good. The identification of these values with the infinite series of their individual expressions fills the soul with a sense of reverence and responsibility towards life, that cannot be equalled by any faith in static, immovable ideals, by which a term, however high and remote, is set to the living spirit, no longer recognised as the creator of its own æsthetic and moral world. To the mind that has grasped this relation of the universal to the individual, of the eternal to the present (and the artist or the saint grasps it in his own unphilosophical way, to which his work or his action is witness), the whole of reality, human and natural, appears as linked by a bond of spiritual solidarity, moving towards the same end, engaged in the same sacred task.

Truth is the value of the logical activity, and therefore it coincides with the positive history of human thought. Its actuality is an infinite progress or development, but not in the sense that the value itself may be subject to increase or change from century to century. At no particular point in that history is it possible to point to a conversion from error to truth, to a total illumination or revelation. Every single affirmation of truth, from the simplest and humblest to the most elaborate and complex, takes possession of the whole of reality, in the fulness of its relations; since it is manifestly impossible to affirm the truth of one individual subject, without implicitly determining its position in the universe. Truth, as all other values, has no extension; it is incommensurable either with space or with time, it is not augmented by accumulation. Degrees in truth, and a more and a less, are inconceivable; but each act that affirms it contains its whole, since truth itself does not live except in the spirit that perpetually creates and recreates it. Truth belongs to the thinking mind, that is, to reality as a logical consciousness, as life belongs to the living body. It belongs to us, individually, in relation to that universal consciousness, in the mode and measure of our partaking of it: which means that however much of it we may conquer, however constant, laborious, honest, intense our efforts towards truth may be, yet our duty towards it will always remain infinite, inexhaustible. The conquered truth is dead in the mind that rests in it, that ceases its effort, as life gives place to death in the body that no longer functions.

In a wider sense, truth belongs to every form of spiritual activity. Beauty, utility, goodness are the truths of the artistic, the practical, the moral mind. And in the actual life of the spirit, each of these values represents all the others in the particular act in which it realizes itself. This is what Croce means by his circular conception of the spirit. And this is why what is said of one value seems to apply without any change to the others; why, as we said elsewhere, all universals are but one universal. Whether we call this one Progress or Development, Spirit or Reality, Mind or Nature, we know that our thought is grasping Life itself, not in its abstract identity, but in its infinite actuality, that is, each time, this life, this beauty, this action, this truth. What we aim at is not an ecstatic absorption into the undifferentiated unity, but the finding within ourselves of a centre of consciousness, capable of introducing order and reason into the variegated spectacle of the natural and human world, not from outside and from above, but from its very heart. The truth that we seek is therefore never external to ourselves, but our own activity, our own life, our own history.

This concept of truth as activity and as history, this activistic and energetic philosophy, truly positive in that the course of history appears to it as a succession of only positive acts and positive values, is not however a blind and fatuous optimism. If it is true that nowhere positive error or positive evil can interrupt the process of life, that death itself does not end but fulfil it, yet from the relations and implications of the various forms of activity arises a real dialectic of good and evil, of truth and error, which is the spring and motive of life. What to the purely utilitarian conscience is the good of now and of to-day, the same conscience, awakened to a greater light, repudiates as evil. The imaginative vision of the poet, in which truth expresses itself, sensuous and finite, and yet pregnant of its infinity, dissolves like mist in the sun in the clearness of the logical concept, and is then restored in its right by the historical and critical consciousness to which that truth is poetry. The myths and superstitions of the old religions, dead in the letter, are revived in the thought itself that seems to destroy them. History is but this perpetual cycle of death and resurrection, in which what is concrete distinction in the act transforms itself into opposition in the process, producing the terms of a new problem and becoming the source of the new creation. Thus the whole method of Croce's philosophy reveals itself as directed towards a realistic conception of life, and the distinctions within the concept are not abstract forms, but the very structure of reality.

The professional philosopher moves always and only in the rarefied atmosphere of the pure concept.

Croce came to philosophy from art and from economics, and he never lost contact with the elementary
forms of knowledge and of action. What might be
termed as his fundamental discoveries are his definitions of the æsthetic and of the economic principle.
On this basis the whole of his thought rests. Without
a conception of a truth which is sufficient unto itself,
and yet is not logical truth, and of a good which has
its own justification, and yet is not moral good, he
would have been compelled to maintain by the side
of the concepts of truth and of goodness, error and
evil as positive realities, or to include the whole of
reality within what would have been truth and goodness in a purely verbal sense. In both cases, he
would have been unable to make his philosophy immediately adherent to all grades of active consciousness, from the lowest to the highest, and thereby to
history. Of these discoveries the one that until
now has attracted the greatest attention is that of
the pure intuition, and of art and language as expression. But the establishment of the economic
principle, that is of the world of nature, of feeling,
of passion, as a positive grade of the spiritual process,
will probably be counted as Croce's greatest achievement, by those who shall be able to look back on his
work with an ampler perspective. It is through it
that his philosophy of the spirit, and in this philosophy, the consciousness of our day, has taken possession of that other world, of that persistent tran-
scendance, which we call nature. In this direction

lies, undoubtedly, the future course of the thought of an age, to which, in this afterglow of a great conflagration, all problems seem to gather into the one of the subjection to its better and higher self, the utilization for its purer purposes, of its own cumbersome economic body, of its nature and of its passions.

BIBLIOGRAPHICAL NOTE

Croce's Complete Works form a collection of twenty-eight volumes, in four distinct series, published by Laterza e Figli, of Bari, who are also the publishers of *La Critica*, and of the following collections initiated or directed by Croce: *Scrittori d'Italia, Scrittori Stranieri, Classici della Filosofia Moderna.*

We give here a full list of the *Opere di Benedetto Croce*, adding to the title of each volume the year of the last available edition, the years of their composition having already been indicated in the text:

Filosofia dello Spirito ("Philosophy of the Spirit"):
> Vol. I, *Estetica*, 1912. (Translated under the title of "Æsthetic.")
> Vol. II, *Logica*, 1917. (Translated under the title of "Logic.")
> Vol. III, *Filosofia della Pratica*, 1915. (Translated under the title of "The Philosophy of the Practical: Economics and Ethics.")
> Vol. IV, *Teoria e Storia della Storiografia*, 1920. (Translated under the title of "Theory and History of Historiography" in England, and under the title of "History: Its Theory and Practice" in the United States.)

Saggi filosofici ("Philosophical Essays"):
> Vol. I, *Problemi di Estetica*, 1910. ("Problems of Æsthetics.")
> Vol. II, *La Filosofia di Giambattista Vico*, 1911. (Translated under the title of "The Philosophy of Vico.")
> Vol. III, *Saggio sullo Hegel*, 1913. ("Essay on Hegel," followed by essays on the history of philosophy; the essay on Hegel translated under the title of "What Is Living and What Is Dead in the Philosophy of Hegel.")
> Vol. IV, *Materialismo Storico ed economia marxistica*, 1918. (Trans-

lated under the title of "Historical Materialism and Marxian Economics.")

Vol. V, *Nuovi Saggi di Estetica*, 1920. ("New Essays on Æsthetics"; contains the *Breviario di Estetica*, translated under the title of "The Essence of Æsthetics.")

Vol. VI, *Frammenti di Etica*, 1922. ("Fragments of Ethics.")

Scritti di Storia letteraria e politica. ("Writings on Literary and Political History"):

Vol. I, *Saggi sulla Letteratura italiana del Seicento*, 1911. ("Essays on Italian Literature in the Seventeenth Century.")

Vol. II, *La Rivoluzione napoletana del 1799*, 1912. ("The Neapolitan Revolution of 1799.")

Vols. III–VI, *La Letteratura della nuova Italia*, 1914–15. "(The Literature of the New Italy.")

Vol. VII, *I Teatri di Napoli*, 1916. ("The Theatres of Naples.")

Vol. VIII, *La Spagna nella Vita italiana durante la Rinascenza*, 1917. ("Spain in Italian Life during the Renaissance.")

Vols. IX–X, *Conversazioni critiche*, 1918. ("Critical Conversations ")

Vol. XI, *Storie e leggende napoletane*, 1919. "(Historical Tales and Legends of Naples.")

Vol. XII, *Goethe*, 1919.

Vol. XIII, *Una Famiglia di Patrioti*, 1919. ("A Family of Patriots"; includes essays on Francesco de Sanctis)

Vol. XIV, *Ariosto, Shakespeare e Corneille*, 1920 (Translated under the title of "Ariosto, Shakespeare, and Corneille.")

Vols. XV–XVI, *Storia della Storiografia italiana*, 1920. ("The History of Italian Historiography.")

Vol. XVII, *La Poesia di Dante*, 1921. ("The Poetry of Dante.")

Scritti varii. ("Miscellaneous Writings"):

Vol. I, *Primi Saggi*, 1919. ("Early Essays ")

The following volumes are not included in the Laterza edition of Croce's works:

Cultura e vita morale, Bari, 1914. ("Culture and Moral Life.")

Aneddoti e profili settecenteschi, Palermo, 1914. ("Anecdotes and Profiles of the Eighteenth Century.")

Contributo alla critica di me stesso, Naples, 1918. ("Contribution to a Criticism of Myself "; one hundred copies printed for private distribution.)

Curiosità storiche, Naples, 1920. ("Historical Curiosities.")

Pagine Sparse, edited by G. Castellano, Naples, 1919–1920. ("Scattered Pages," consisting of *Pagine di letteratura e di cultura*, 2 vols ; *Pagine sulla guerra;* and *Memorie, scritti biografici e appunti storici.*)

A complete bibliography, cataloguing the whole of Croce's multifarious activity, is outside the scope of this note. The nearest approach to it can be found in G. Castellano's *Introduzione alle opere di B. Croce*, Bari, 1920, which contains, besides, a full list of translations in eight languages, a bibliography of the Italian and foreign critical literature on Croce, and a very useful series of abstracts of discussions and judgments on Croce's work.

Besides articles and essays in American and English magazines and reviews, the following works of Croce have been translated into English: the four volumes of the *Filosofia dello Spirito*, the essay on Hegel, the *Essence of Æsthetics*, and the essays on *Ariosto, Shakespeare, and Corneille*, by Douglas Ainslie; the essay on Vico, by R. G. Collingwood, and the essays on Historical Materialism, by C. M. Meredith. But the English or American student of Croce ought to rely as little as possible on translations; the reading of the Italian text will be found comparatively easy, on the basis of a good acquaintance with Latin or with French. The labour entailed by the surmounting of the first difficulties will be largely repaid by the advantages gained in coming into direct contact with Croce's thought, and by the acquisition of at least a reading knowledge of Italian.

For the vast critical literature on Croce, scattered through the literary and philosophical reviews of Europe and of America during the last twenty years, we are compelled again to refer the reader to Castellano's book. We shall only mark out Croce's own autobiographical notes, the *Contributo* listed above, which, however, having been printed for private circulation only, is not generally accessible except in the French translation printed in the *Revue de Métaphysique et de Morale*, XXVI, pp. 1–40. The following are the only books which give a general view of Croce's thought: G. Prezzolini, *Benedetto Croce*, Naples, 1909; E. Chiocchetti, *La filosofia di B. Croce*, Florence, 1915; H. Wildon Carr, *The Philosophy of B. Croce*, London, 1917. The first is an able, but very cursory sketch; the second examines Croce's philosophy from the standpoint of neoscholasticism; the third is an ample summary written by a distinguished writer well acquainted with the various currents of modern thought. Each of them ought to be read with a critical and discriminating eye.

In the English-speaking world, Croce's fame rests emphatically on his æsthetics, and its applications to literary criticism. His influence on English and American critical thought has already gone much deeper than a mere list of writings on his theories would show; especially in England, his ideas are, so to speak, in the air, and appear in many writers who have no direct knowledge of his work. The best exposition of this phase of his philosophy is to be found in E. F. Carritt's book, *The Theory of Beauty*, 1914, chap. XIV. The writings of A. B. Walkley, and of J. E. Spingarn, contain the most vigorous prosecution of his thought as applied, respectively, to English and to American scholarship and criticism.

For the general history of Italian thought, to which many a reference is made in the course of this book, the best helps, besides Croce's essay on Vico, and B. Spaventa, *La filosofia italiana*, recently reprinted, Bari, 1909, are the historical works of Giovanni Gentile, and especially his *Storia della filosofia italiana*, Milano, n. d. Gentile is one of the most profound and earnest modern European thinkers, and it is desirable that his theoretical works, similar in tendency to, but widely divergent in temper from those of Croce, should become better known to the Anglo-Saxon world. Two of his books, *La Riforma dell' Educazione* and *Teoria generale dello Spirito*, are soon to appear in English. Croce's judgment on Gentile's Actual Idealism is expressed in *Una discussione tra filosofi amici*, in *Conversazioni Critiche*, II, pp. 67–95. But a complete understanding of the vital relations between the two thinkers can be gathered only through an adequate knowledge of both Croce's and Gentile's work.

INDEX

A priori synthesis, 157, 199
Absolute, 156
Abstractions, 292
Accademia Pontaniana, 45
Action, thought versus, 188, volition identified with, 194
Activity, æsthetic and practical, relations, 126; theoretical and practical, 117
Æsthetic criticism, 135, 136
Æsthetic personality, 282
Æsthetic principle, 303
Æsthetic production, 124
Æesthetic standards, 137, 138
Æsthetic value, 128
Æsthetics, 100, Croce's theory, 49, German, 63, 65, hedonistic theories, 127; importance in Croce's thought, 63, theories and doctrines, 118; Vico's influence on Croce, 53–54
Agnosticism, 263
American philosophy and culture, 21
Aristotle, 215
Art, as expression, 108; concept, 49, 116, history as an art, 47, literary and rhetorical criticism of, 137; morality and, 121, 126, 279; object, 123, 127; science and, 53; technique and, 130, universality,, 277
Artist's personality, 282
Arts, particular, 132
Asceticism, 213
Avenarius, 144

Beauty, 49; as an end in itself, 123; natural, 51, 127; objective, 127
Becoming, 151, 206

Bergson, Henri, 171, 295; on free will, 198, resemblance to Croce, 200
Biography, 59, 61, 282
Bruno, Giordano, 33, 35, 151, 185, 293, 294
Byron, 140

Campanella, Tomaso, 33, 35
Capitalist society, 77, 81
Carducci, Giosuè, 23, 26
Chronicle, 257
Classicism, 281
Classification, 156
Comte, Auguste, 179
Concept, 101, 105; as a unity of distinctions, 149; expression and, 154, identity of pure concept with individual judgment, 156; language and, 111; logical, 145, 146, pure concept, 141, 146, 160; two forms, 155; universal, particular and singular, 150
Conceptual fictions, 146
Consciousness, 190, 206
Contemporaneity, 255
Content and form, 108, 109
Copernicus, 35
Creation, 286, 288
Critic, 287, 288
Critica, La, 95, 247
Criticism, æsthetic, theory, 135; history and, 274; monographic method, 283; technique and, 130, *see also* Literary criticism
Criticism of life, 139
Croce, Benedetto, activities in 1900–1910, 93, æsthetic theory, 49, approach to philosophy and method of work, 28; bibli-

311

163, 265, 287; monographic method, 286, object, 270; of man and of nature, 271; philological, 259; philosophy of, 180, poetical, 261; positivity, 269, problem of, 13; return to, and elaboration of the theory, 247, rhetorical, 261; science and, 168, special histories, 271, spirit as history, 258, theory of, 253; thought and, 262, 265, two meanings of the word, 253, universal, 264, 265

Idealism, 41; transcendental, 290
Ideals, function, 202
Immanentism, 100–101, 152
Immortality, 206
Impressionism, 281
Individual, society and, 226; universal and, 222
Individual judgment, 155
Individuality, 204
Industrial revolution, 76
Inquisition, 177
Inspiration, 123, 132
Intellect, 148
Intention, action and, 162; volition and, 194
Intuition, 101, Croce's use of the word, 112; identification with expression, 106, kinds, 107, lyrical character, 114
Intuitive consciousness, 102
Intuitive knowledge, limits, 104, 105

Judgment, æsthetic, 136; individual, 155, kinds, 155, 156, practical, 196
Jus naturale, 232

Kant, 37, 61, 142, 143, 182; ethics, 83
Knowledge, forms, 101, 159; will and, 193

Labriola, Antonio, influence on Croce, 8; on Marxism and materialism, 71

Language, law and, 237, origin and nature, 110, 280, technique of, 134
Law, definition, 228, language and, 237, mutability of laws, 231; philosophy of, 227, 236, social and individual, 229, use of laws, 233
Law of nature, 232
Legalism, 234
Liberty and necessity, 199
Literary criticism, definition, 58; problem of, 57, three phases, 60
Literary critics and art, 137
Literary genre, 133
Logic, 67, 81, 100, 106, 244; function in Croce's system, 141
Logical concept, 145–146

Mach, E, 144
Machiavelli, 83, 215,
Marxism, 21, Croce's interest, 71; influence on Croce, 215; morality and, 82
Materialism, historical, 71; criticism and interpretation, 75
Mathematical thought, 171, 217
Mathematicism, 179
Mechanists, 170
Metaphysics, 157, 268
Methodology, philosophy as, 268
Moral concepts, 66
Moral standards, 202
Moralism, abstract, 211
Morality, 208, 223; art and, 121, 126; Marxism and, 82, utility and, 212
Mysticism, 183
Myth, 182
Mythologism, 182

National prejudices, 176
Nationality, 232
Natural laws, 230
Natural rights, 232
Natural sciences, 167
Naturalism, 33, 40, 291

CPSIA information can be obtained
at www.ICGtesting.com
Printed in the USA
BVHW05s1829300418
514824BV00017B/427/P

9 781332 598342